IMMIGRANTS!
Latino Voices in a Time of Turmoil

Jane Lubart draws on 20 years of political experience in Washington, D.C., and 16 years of teaching English to adult immigrants in Washington State to give us a compelling account of immigration in the United States today.

PRAISE FOR *IMMIGRANTS!*

"Very well done! *Immigrants! Latino Voices in a Time of Turmoil* is a pleasure to read. It greatly adds to our knowledge of how immigrants add to the special qualities that make up America.
Highly recommend Jane Lubart's book that looks beyond the headlines to show how real immigrants - the new face of America today and tomorrow - are like our ancestors who came to America from Europe. Today's immigrants are no different as they are still pursuing the American Dream and helping our country's diverse future."
-Robert Guttman, Editor-in-Chief, TransAtlantic Magazine.com and Professor of American Politics at Johns Hopkins University and University of Virginia.

"This book is needed and will be very valuable in the struggle to gain respect for immigrants."
-Alma Flor Ada, author, *Gathering the Sun*

Dillo Publications
2019

MORE PRAISE FOR *IMMIGRANTS!*

"I love this book. As a filmmaker, I appreciated the vivid and deeply personal portrayals of the immigrants. Congratulations on a very enjoyable and meaningful book."
--Sally Rosenthal, Emmy Award Winning Film Producer

Dillo Publications
2019

IMMIGRANTS!
Latino Voices in a Time of Turmoil

By Jane Lubart

Dillo Publications
Seattle Washington

For My Students, My Heroes

DISCLAIMER

This book is based on interviews with my students. The views and opinions expressed are those of the characters only and do not necessarily represent the views and opinions held by the individuals on whose characters the stories are based.

ACKNOWLEDGEMENTS

First and foremost, I acknowledge all the students I have been privileged to teach. They number well over a thousand and each and every one taught me more than I could ever acknowledge. This book is about people from Latin America, but although Latinos are by far the majority of my students, they are by no means the only ones.

I will never forget the young men who braved harrowing trips out of Eritrea. They were packed in unimaginable numbers into cars to speed across the desert, and they somehow survived leaky boats across the Mediterranean. I acknowledge the Laotian gentleman who fought on the side of the United States. He was tattooed head to foot to identify him and prevent his leaving, but he left nonetheless and raised his family in America. I acknowledge the Russian man who fought in the Russian army in Afghanistan for seven years without a day off.

These events were vividly brought home to me night after night in my classroom. I couldn't include all their stories, but they are forever with me. Stories of terrible poverty, torture, death and dismemberment haunt me. Through it all somehow my students retained their hope, their dreams, and their humanity. They are my heroes.

I especially acknowledge the help I've had along the way. Ruth Meacham has been my friend, my mentor, my inspiration, and my editor. William Enriquez spurred me on to interview the students and helped immeasurably with translations and insights. Andrea Rosenthal helped with many of the wonderful photographs. Dylan Becker read drafts and offered invaluable criticism. Noah Wittner provided artistic advice.

I especially thank Alma Flor Ada and her publisher, Harper Collins, for the poems from her book, **Gathering the Sun,** which begin the chapters of immigrant stories.

Finally, I want to deeply thank Norman L. Green of Threshold Documents for his invaluable assistance in getting this manuscript to publication.

Contents

INTRODUCTION

"The bosom of America is open to receive
not only the Opulent and respectable Stranger,
but the oppressed and persecuted of
all Nations and Religions."
President George Washington

My motivation to teach English to immigrants and to write this book came from my grandparents who left their families in Eastern Europe for the United States in 1905. They braved overloaded, disease-plagued boats to avoid persecution and death in their home countries. They were teenagers, the first in their families to make the trip, and their whole lives were ahead of them. They told me that as they neared Ellis Island and saw the Statue of Liberty, they felt the long, difficult and lonely journey had been worth it. It was as if the words inscribed on the Statue of Liberty were written for them: "Give me your tired, your poor,

1

your huddled masses yearning to breathe free." Certainly, my grandparents qualified on all counts. They settled in America and never looked back

What greeted my grandparents were low paying jobs in substandard workplaces, bad, overcrowded housing, a new language and strange customs, and, to make it all more difficult, xenophobia. What saved them and countless other immigrants were a determination to succeed, some might even say desperation, and a society that, for all its detractions, rewarded hard work and talent.

Each wave of immigrants faces hardship and xenophobia in much the same way. They are busy trying to survive, to get ahead, to raise families and finally to assimilate. They don't have the luxury or time to let difficulties and xenophobia deter them from their goals.

I have had the privilege of teaching English as a Second Language to adult immigrants at a local community college for the past 16 years. Quarter after academic quarter, I am impressed that so many people come to learn English after a hard day's work and family obligations. We study for two and a half hours a night, four nights a week. At the beginning of each quarter and at the end, the college administers a standardized test to measure progress. Even those who enter my beginning English class with little or no education in their home countries make astonishing progress. They can read, write, speak and understand a great deal of English after only a few months of attending class.

This short book is based on the stories from the students in my classes. It is not an unbiased account. I am definitely on their side as they bravely adjust to a new country, a new language and a new way of life.

Immigration: Then and Now

We may be a nation of nations, but immigration has been problematic from the start. The Founding Fathers settled in 17th century Massachusetts in search of religious freedom. They promptly tried to pull up the gangplank behind them. Tolerance was not exactly the way of newcomers to America either towards the Native Americans who had been here for at least 12,000 years before them or subsequent immigrants who sought to make the new world their home as well.

America's attitude towards new waves of arrivals has been very well documented. From "The Truth about Immigrants" by Brian Frazelle to "American Xenophobia" about Jefferson's election by Tom Heath to "Anger: An American History" by Stacey Schiff, journalists, historians, and politicians have chronicled the country's treatment of immigrants and Native Americans.

It may come as a surprise to some that even English and Scottish immigrants were much maligned during the pro-French wave which brought Thomas Jefferson, former U.S. Ambassador to France and a Francophile, into the Presidency. And so it went with the national groups that followed. From the Germans, to the Italians, to the Chinese, to the east Indians, the Irish and others, xenophobia comingled with the American dream.

America's complicated and sometimes contradictory treatment of immigrants from our neighbors to the South is no exception. The United States shares a 1,989 mile border with Mexico. As part of the settlement of the 1846-1848 Mexican-American War, the border moved south and encompassed what is now California, Nevada, New Mexico, Utah, most of Arizona and Colorado and parts of Texas, Oklahoma, Kansas and Wyoming. Those living in what had been part of Mexico did not so much emigrate to what would become the United States as they were surrounded.

In his book, **Illegal People,** author and photojournalist David Bacon tells us: "For centuries there were no visas or 'papers' needed in order to enter the United States, and anyone could walk across the border. It's still only a minor civil violation to be in the country without documents. 'Illegal' is all about social and political status."

In 1994, the year the North American Free Trade Agreement (NAFTA) went into effect, crossing was still relatively easy. President Salinas of Mexico sold NAFTA to his people by saying it would reduce the need to migrate by providing more employment at home. Ray Suarez in his book, **Latino Americans,** disputes the claim that NAFTA reduced migration when, instead, it "brought prosperity to metropolitan areas while making it harder to earn a living on the land."

In fact, for years following NAFTA, immigration from Mexico surged. Under the terms of the trade agreement, large American corn producers were allowed to 'dump' corn in Mexico, and it became cheaper to import corn than grow it in Mexico. Two million Mexican farmers went out of business, many of them in the poorer states of Oaxaca and Chiapas.

David Bacon noted, "NAFTA became an accelerant, pouring gasoline on the fire of economic reform. Instead of creating prosperity, it displaced workers and farmers at an even greater rate…By 2010 half the country's population was living in poverty with about 20 percent living in extreme poverty." Economic desperation meant migration to other parts of Mexico and the United States, and remittances home became a lifeline and a way of life.

The number of Mexicans living in the United States went from 4.5 million in 1990 to more than double that number in 2000. In 2008, it peaked at 12.67 million.

Who are they and why did they come? What did they do once they got here? In brief, meet twelve individuals whose stories represent different aspects of the current immigration picture. All but two are from Mexico. Some are undocumented while others entered the United States under a variety of visas. Their histories are subsequently presented in greater depth in this book.

Meet the Immigrants

Child Bride: Mireya crossed the border with a lecherous coyote (guide) because her father sold her into marriage. She was a child of 14 and found herself in a new country with a much older husband who turned out to have already married someone else.

Born in the U.S.A.: William was born in the United States, a citizen by birth, only to leave before he was even a toddler to be raised in Guadalajara, Mexico. He returned to excel and graduate from university with high honors. Mexico's loss is our gain.

Dreamer: Beatriz came as a child with her mom on a tourist visa, and her family stayed. Beatriz and her whole family worked in the fields of California and Washington State. She attained a university degree, but because of her undocumented status, she thought her dream of becoming a teacher was beyond her grasp. Today, thanks to the Deferred Action for Childhood Arrivals or DACA program (quickly dubbed the 'dreamers' program), Beatriz' life and dream begin.

Rite of Passage: Fernando crossed the border on foot. He picks, plants, packs and ships the flowers that make this part of the country famous. He sought adventure and opportunity and found romance and family.

The Overstayer: Rosa fled violence and uncertainty in Peru and entered the United States as a tourist. She married an American and devotes her life to giving back to the community. She accomplished her goal of higher education.

A Love Story: Martin crossed the border many years ago and never looked back. He gained legal status under President Reagan's amnesty program and made a life here in the States.

A Love Story: Maria followed her heart and joined Martin as his fiancé and then as his wife. True love and a new country greeted her.

The Affluent Immigrant: Jorge could not find a job in northern Mexico in spite of university and technical training in robotics. He fled discrimination on a tourist visa and found freedom.

Amnesty's Child: Carmen was placed inside a small coffin and smuggled across the border when she was 12. Against great odds, she accomplished the nearly impossible, nursing assistant professional certification, a big step on her way towards a dream of becoming a nurse.

Remittance Man: Eduardo survived an upbringing in an orphanage to be reunited with his family. He journeyed, not once but twice, to the country in the north in order to support his mother, sister and daughter. Even his dog, Feroz, grows comfortable on remittances.

Farmworker: Jesus wanted to stay in Oaxaca, Mexico, but his family needed his earnings from the United States. He uncomplainingly worked hard at farm labor only to become embroiled in a labor dispute that drew national attention.

A Man for the Poor: The Padre was on his way to a posting in Africa from ministering to the faithful in his native Colombia when America made him an offer. He's been here ever since, and his contribution to the Catholic Church in Washington is immeasurable. Now he is a U.S. citizen, and his devotion to the poor and vulnerable continues.

CHAPTER 1
CHILD BRIDE MIREYA

Watering
Your smiles
To your friends
Are like water
To growing plants

Alma Flor Ada

Mireya was a carefree girl in her hometown of Veracruz who never made a conscious decision to go to the United States. Her family, she knew, was poor, but then much of Mexico's entire population lives in poverty. By comparison, her life was all right. Her father grew mangos, oranges, avocados and all kinds of chili peppers and vegetables, and she never went hungry. But life in Veracruz was difficult for the family because there were very few jobs available.

Situated on the Gulf of Mexico, Veracruz is the country's largest, oldest and most important port. The city is famous for the eponymous 1954 movie, *Vera Cruz*, starring Burt Lancaster and Gary Cooper, and tourists flock to its beaches.

The song "La Bamba, "made popular by Ritchie Valens, represents the city's Afro-Caribbean style. It is a vibrant city of music, dancing and life. However, for people like Mireya and her family, it is a place without a bright future.

Child Bride

"A month after I turned 14, my dad came to me and said it was time for me to get married. He knew someone who wanted to marry me. According to my dad he was a good person and would take care of me. The only problem was that I would have to go to America because the man who would become my husband lived and worked there. He had seen me and wanted me for his wife. I don't know how much he paid my father for me, but I didn't have a choice. I had to marry this man who was 23 years older than me."

Despite her husband's legal status in the U.S., Mireya was forced to cross the border illegally.

Child marriages are fairly common in Mexico. Although the legal age of consent is 18, many parents allow their daughters to marry earlier. By age 18, over one-fifth of women are married, and about 5 percent are married before the age of 15. Problems of child marriage have undoubtedly

9

grown worse as a result of internet ads for 'Hot Mexican Brides,' 'Secret Resorts in Mexico' and 'Images for Child Brides.'

Happy Childhood to Forced Marriage

Before her early marriage, Mireya remembers being happy in Veracruz. Kids there can do whatever they want and go everywhere. "My sister, brothers and I had fun. We were poor but free," she recalled. This sentiment was a common refrain among the students I interviewed.

Mireya is a beautiful woman and must have been a very pretty teenager. When she walked into the classroom, heads would turn. When she smiled, she lit up the room. One night she arrived dressed up and announced that she was going out after class. She was wearing a low-cut, tight black dress that showed off her elegant presence. It is likely that many of the men had trouble concentrating that night.

I try to imagine this young Caribbean/Mexican beauty as a teenager running through the desert to a new country and an unknown fate. She recalls the shock to find herself alone with seven men and no girls or women. Mireya was supposed to meet her husband on the other side of the border. She ran for miles; soaking with sweat, she had to sleep in the desert. In the middle of the night, the coyote, the man paid to escort her safely from Mexico to the United States, tried to rape her. She screamed and ran to her companions. They understood what was happening and took care of her.

"They formed a circle around me, and I slept in the middle. They weren't about to let harm come to me," she said.

It took her a week to find her husband after she crossed the border.

"I had no money and no place to stay. I knew no English. I was scared and lost in a strange country. When I finally found my husband, we went to Idaho. My sister had gone there before me, and we stayed with her and her family. But then things went bad. My sister's husband tried to do things with me, and we couldn't stay at my sister's anymore. I found an apartment for us, and we lived in Idaho for three years," she said.

Mireya felt so young, not like a wife at all, more like her husband's daughter.

Early Married Life: A Shocking Surprise

As in Veracruz, jobs in Idaho were scarce, so Mireya and her husband moved to Washington State where he got a job in a large commercial chicken operation. They lived on the farm, and Mireya worked there too for a short time. Companies like this hire people and let them work for a season or two. Then they check a worker's immigration status and fire them if it comes back questionable. Once Mireya's lack of documentation was known, the company let her go.

"After that, I wanted papers so that I could work legally. The shock came when I found out that my husband was already married to someone who was also in the U.S. Someone else had already received legal status because of him. "

"But I didn't give up. It was bad enough to be a wife to him, but I could not accept that he was a bigamist. I wanted my papers. He got really mad because he knew it meant that he would have to divorce his other wife. I stood my ground. There were many, many fights, but I found a lawyer for free. It took five years, but he finally divorced his first wife, and I got my papers," Mireya proudly told me.

"Once my immigration status was fixed, I realized I could visit my family in Mexico. I was really lonely for them. By then, I had two children, and my mother and father had never seen them. I left Mexico a girl and came back a mother, *senorita to senora*. When I saw my parents and my brothers, I cried and cried. When I told them the whole story, how my so-called husband was married to someone else, my father felt really bad. He was a broken man by then and died shortly after my visit."

Mireya didn't want to return to the United States, but she knew she must. She had two children, a daughter and a son, and no way to support them in Mexico.

Heinous Acts

The real trouble started one fateful night. Mireya was in bed when she heard her daughter crying, at first softly, then sobbing. Her daughter was eleven years old. Mireya got up, went to the other room and saw her husband standing over her daughter with his pants down.

Right there and then Mireya wanted a divorce. "I never loved my husband. It wasn't just that he was so much older than me. It was because he was mean. And when I saw what he did to my daughter, I hated him and wanted a divorce. Things like this happen in Mexico, and very often women don't have a choice. But this was America, and I had a choice. I knew that I could be free and support my children, and that I didn't have to be in the marriage anymore. I had a job, and I had confidence. In Mexico not many people got a divorce at that time, but I wasn't in Mexico anymore, and I didn't want to be married to a mean, abusive man who was so much older than me," she explained. "I had to save my daughter."

At first, her husband didn't consent to the divorce. Then, he said he would give her a divorce but no child support. She said OK that she would support her kids by herself. She found a house to rent and tried to move out with her two children. "My husband said he would kill me. Then changing his tune, he said someone at my work wanted to kill me, but I didn't buy it because I had no problems at work. He threatened me, 'you move out today, and you'll see what happens tomorrow.'"

Free at Last

Mireya was afraid of him and called the police. "The cops helped me move out. They only let me take clothes for my kids. They said I should watch out tonight. I asked them to watch my house because I had to go to work that night."

Sure enough, around one in the morning, Mireya got a call from the police. Her new rental house had been burned to the ground, and now she had nothing. The cops knew her husband did it, but when they looked for him, he was nowhere to be found.

"He ran away to Mexico, and we never saw him again. I am so happy because my kids were not in the house that night. They went to spend the night at the babysitter's. Usually, the babysitter would spend the night at my house, but that night she couldn't. That was our good luck because otherwise, everyone might be dead."

Mireya's life was turned upside down for a long time. Her daughter was so upset that she couldn't go to school for a month, but Mireya had to go to work no matter what. People contributed to help her out bringing her clothes and essentials. The Red Cross paid for a motel for three months until she could find another place to live. She was on her own now. From being a 14-year-old bride to a young mother, somehow she found the strength to start over.

Starting Over

"I haven't heard from my husband since that night. Right now he owes $30,000 in child support. Someone in Mexico said he had a bad disease, so he may already be dead. He would be 65. When I married him he was 42. To get social security survivor benefits for my children, they say I must bring a death certificate. He may be in Tijuana as he has a big family there, but nobody knows what happened to him, or nobody is saying."

From time to time, the police come and question Mireya about her husband's whereabouts. He is suspected of arson and perhaps attempted murder. They would like to find him and bring him back to the United States. So far, he remains a fugitive, if he is still alive.

Mireya's son is disabled for life and needs the social security survivor benefits. He was born with fragile bones and has to go to Children's Hospital in Seattle every three months for a checkup. He needs medication and goes to a special school.

"He is a good boy and has a good attitude. But he has to be careful not to lose weight or his bones will have problems. He eats a lot but is still skinny," Mireya said.

Mireya herself came to my class while she was on disability (known as Labor and Industries' disability in Washington State or L&I). Like many immigrants, she did dangerous factory work and was injured on the job. Latinos comprise 15 percent of the labor force but account for 20 percent of the workplace fatalities. And, even as fatal work injury rates decline for the working population as a whole, they are increasing for Latino workers. Nonfatal injuries are on the rise too, especially falls.

"I fell down and broke my shoulder in three places. I was working in seafood processing, and the floor was very slippery from the fish. I fell on the factory floor. I worked there for seven years, but the company didn't want to pay me. I got a lawyer, and the lawyer fought for me to get L&I compensation for five years. I am still in pain from that injury, and the doctors say I need another operation, but I can't afford more surgery. I already had three operations on my shoulder."

Mireya used her time on disability to attend English classes. Even though she lived 45 minutes from the college, she showed up every night, on time, eager to learn. She made great progress and could have easily continued to get her high school diploma and special training. When the disability pay ran out, she had to return to working long hours.

Dreams for the Future

"I got a lump-sum settlement of $5,000 because of my disability. I took that money and my tax refund to start a business in Veracruz. My brother is in charge of our business making tortillas. The tortilla machine runs every day. We have six workers and one who delivers the tortillas by motorcycle. The workers are paid about $60 a week. My dream is to build a house in Mexico," Mireya gladly tells the story.

There are a lot of things Mireya likes about the United States. In many ways, she grew up here. She found opportunities to study and help her children who were born here. "My daughter just graduated from high school, and she wants to be a veterinarian. She likes the idea of living in Mexico and having chickens and cows around. She and I went through a lot, but the most important thing is that we are happy now, and we have a good life."

"For me, the most difficult part of being in the United States is the language. Some people are mean to Mexicans and make fun of our English. But what I see is that it's difficult for everyone here, Mexicans and everyone else. We are all struggling."

Mireya gets up at 3 a.m. five days a week to commute to her job at a department store. Early in the morning, long before customers arrive, she sorts the new merchandise, tags it in the warehouse space and gets it ready for sale.

She sees her life as free of problems. "I hear there are a lot of problems in the high schools with alcohol and drugs, but not my daughter. She sees that I don't drink, or do drugs. My daughter remembers everything from growing up and is writing a book about it. It is not a pretty picture. It's sad that she went through so much, but I think she is strong, and she can keep going."

From the beginning of the quarter, Mireya's daughter accompanied her mother to class. She would sit next to her mother and do her high school homework. From time to time, she would help us with translations when we needed them. She is attending community college.

A final note on Mireya's story. Her daughter will graduate from community college in the Spring with a nursing degree. Mireya herself begins a job with the State of Washington helping other families who have children with disabilities.

CHAPTER 2

BORN IN THE U.S.A. WILLIAM

Mexico
My grandparents
Came from Mexico
My parents
Returned to Mexico.
My dream is
To visit Mexico,
And you,
What is your dream?

Alma Flor Ada

William appeared in my classroom in the summer of 2008. He sat in the front of the room and paid close attention. He had only recently arrived from Guadalajara, Mexico, and was staying with friends of the family. William was a good student, but it was a class of good students, and I didn't take any particular note of him at the time.

It was only later that I realized how extraordinary he was. In 2010 he was assigned to help me in class, and at first, I didn't recognize him. Only two years before, he had been a student in my beginning English class. Now he was completing his community college course work and was in the process of transferring to the university in the next town.

William is a natural born teacher. From the minute he walked into the classroom, he intuitively knew how to help the students. He would circulate effortlessly offering translations from English to Spanish, explaining grammar points and offering encouragement. I gave him more and more responsibility in front of the class, and he assumed it seamlessly.

I was curious about William's story. How did he go from being a beginning language learner to an accomplished college student in such a short period of time? What was his past? What were his dreams?

Understanding William

William told me, "To understand me, you have to know my dad."

William's dad, Jose Luis, was born into an unfortunate family. Jose Luis' father died when he was eight, and his mom went to live with another man. She didn't feel she could take him with her. It is a difficult aspect of Mexican culture (and others) that men often don't want to raise children from another father, especially male offspring.

A distant cousin offered to take Jose Luis in. The cousin lived in Polanco, the oldest barrio in Guadalajara, a very poor part of town, and had a wife and six children. Young Jose Luis was another mouth to feed, and, although he was only eight years old, he was expected to contribute financially to the family.

As a child who should have been in primary school, Jose Luis went instead to the market to buy flowers, small packages of jello, whatever he could resell in the zocalo. He was a lonely boy who darted about unseen waiting at the side of the market to get the best deals. Then he'd try to make a few pesos selling what he could.

Jose Luis' favorite was to buy flowers, partly because the flowers were beautiful and smelled wonderful to a young boy from the barrio, but primarily because of the flower seller. The flower seller started to save the best flowers for him and often put in extras so he could make more money. It didn't matter to him that she was a young woman of twenty and he was just a boy. By the time he was about 12 years old, he recognized his feelings for the flower seller as romantic love.

Finally, when he was a young man of 17, Jose Luis announced his love to the flower seller. She smiled and said she loved him too. He told her he was going to the United States to earn more money, and then he was coming back to marry her. She was almost 30 then and a single mom living within a large, extended family. He was poor, a good foot shorter than she was, and basically an orphan. But she said yes, she would wait for him to return. He promised to raise her daughter as his own.

North through the Underground Highway

Crossing the border in those days was relatively easy. William's dad went to Tijuana and slipped through sewers buried under the border forming an underground highway north.

He never wavered in his love. Finally, after five years, Jose Luis returned to Guadalajara. Jose Luis and his beloved flower seller were married. The wedding was a joyous affair. William's mom wore a beautiful white dress, and she was surrounded by a loving and attentive family. Jose Luis was there alone since he had long since lost touch with his cousin and the rest of his family. He was in formal dress. They met in the Catholic Church where she had grown up. Jose Luis was a stranger to church, but he did his best to look like he belonged. He saved his money from the United States, and spent it lavishly on a beautiful wedding complete with flowers, bridesmaids, and a gold ring. The celebration after the ceremony was a feast of Mexican specialties.

After a proper sendoff, the couple spent their honeymoon crossing back into the United States to live in Los Angeles. They were married in May, and William and his twin sister, arrived in December. They were born in L.A. with full U.S. citizenship.

'Anchor Babies'

Some might use the term 'anchor babies' to describe William and his sister. They are American because the Fourteenth Amendment to the U.S. Constitution states: "All persons born or naturalized in the U.S. and subject to the jurisdiction thereof are citizens of the United States and of the State wherein they reside." The word "anchor" is used because when these children turn 21 they can, under highly-prescribed terms, sponsor their parents for legal entry into the country.

Generally speaking, the 'anchor baby' term is pejorative. It has been used by some, notably by those who are anti-immigrant, to denote a scheme by foreigners to gain U.S. citizenship. It smacks of pre-planning and conspiracy.

However, researchers have concluded that there "is little evidence to suggest that significant numbers of Latinas are crossing the border to give birth." Having American-born children does not entitle parents to special benefits, nor does it confer legal status on undocumented immigrant parents.

All that said, there are circumstances under which U.S. born children can sponsor their parents when they turn 21. In order to enter the United States two decades and a year after your child is born, you must adhere to stringent rules. For those willing to follow these rules and plan very far ahead, there are even so-called maternity hotels catering to pregnant women from abroad who are waiting to give birth in the U.S. Mostly their clients are the wealthy from Asia and other parts of the world.

William and his twin sister did eventually sponsor their parents, but the designation as *anchors* doesn't really apply. In the first place, their parents did not deliberately cross the border with the intention of giving birth to U.S. citizens. Their father had been here for years working, and they had every intention of making the United States their home for the foreseeable future. Remember, in the years before 2001, entry into the country was relatively easy. Moreover, William's parents had been living outside the country for many, many years before William and his twin applied to sponsor them.

Why didn't William's parents stay in the country as they intended? Why did they return to Mexico?

"My father worked all the time," William recalls. "He was obsessed with providing for his new family. My dad decided that we wouldn't want for anything as he had wanted for almost everything. The only problem was that my mom was very, very unhappy. These days they might call it postpartum depression. She just felt lonely for her family in Mexico. Every night my father would come home exhausted only to find his bride and new mother of his twin babies in tears."

Return to Guadalajara

"When I was two months old, we moved back to Guadalajara. My mother comes from a family of nine brothers and sisters. My sisters and I were loved by so many aunts, uncles, grandparents, and cousins, and my mother was happy again. It wasn't just that she was happy to be back with her family in Mexico. In the United States, we were living in a U.S.-style barrio where gangs ruled. My mother was afraid to leave the house. And, with twins and an older child to contend with, it was no easy thing to even go to the corner market. My father was rarely available to help with daily chores, and my mother had to confront her fears of the neighborhood every time she left the house."

"My memories of growing up in Mexico are good. The only memory I don't have is of my father. He was an invisible force in our house, always working, always. He left the house in the morning before I woke up and returned after I went to sleep. I knew he was providing for us, providing so that we could go to school and have the things he never did. Still, there was a place in my heart that was empty and longed for him."

When William was eight, they moved to what could be termed Guadalajara's suburbs. There were no paved roads there at that time, and the children played outside from morning until night, unfettered by adult supervision. William's life revolved around school, church, family and play.

"When I was around 14, I remember wanting to be a priest. All our family holidays and gatherings were also religious events. I was an altar boy, and I wanted to serve God. But then I was pulled to secular life at a regular school where I loved studying, and by high school, I had a girlfriend, and all thoughts of the priesthood were gone."

Cultural Norms:

Mexico v. the United States

When I first started teaching, I would make a point of asking students what were their dreams. We would sing the Abba song, "I Have a Dream" and write about what we wanted for the future. In almost all cases, the dreams were to help their families, families still in Mexico or other countries and families who'd made it to the United States. Sometimes students would say they wanted a better job or a bigger place to live, but the reasons behind these goals were invariably to give more to their families.

I couldn't help but think of American kids, my own kids. We are one "me generation" after another raised to think highly of ourselves, merited or not, full of dreams for the future, realistic or not. I wondered more than once how American students would answer the question, 'what is your dream?'

William explained why Mexican offspring are so focused on providing for their families. "Even though I didn't grow up in poverty, I always knew we weren't far from it. True, my father went off to work, and my mother stayed home to take care of us children. In some ways, it was like an American middle class family. We lived outside the city, and I attended school. But we always had a connection to our past, a connection to the pueblo where our families came from and the hard poverty of subsistence living. Of course, we knew that there was no safety net, no government program if things went wrong. We depended on family."

"It was a given that my family wanted me to succeed which was why I was in school and not selling flowers in the zocalo. However, I was taught from my earliest memory that whatever I did, however much money I made, it was to share with the family. My importance was not self-importance; rather, it was a feeling of importance to my family."

"For example, in high school I took a job in telemarketing. I worked part time after school, usually from about two in the afternoon to 6:30 or 7:00. I was pretty good at it and made more than the average full-time worker there. But every payday, I gave my money to my mother. It was for the family. There was never any question that the money was only mine to do with as I pleased."

Change: A Move Away from Home

Change arrived when William's dad lost his job. It was not long after the peso collapse of the mid-1990s when jobs were very scarce throughout Mexico.

William's mom and dad started a little store in the neighborhood. Fortunately, they had saved some money and put their savings into the store. Everyone in the family, William included, was expected to work in the store. "Even when I was already in college in the U.S., I would still go home and help my mom in the store when I could. That meant summers stocking shelves, waiting on customers and lifting the heavy things my mother couldn't.

"I'm not sure it was the hardship brought on by my father's job loss or whether I was simply ready for a change. Bad job prospects in Guadalajara played into my thinking. Whatever the cause, when I was a senior in high school, I determined to move north."

Although no one discussed it, William knew that he had been born in the United States and was an American citizen by birth. William announced to his mother that he was going to leave for America. She didn't object because she knew that there was no future for him in Mexico, and she had no money to give him, only her prayers.

North through Tijuana

William went to Tijuana to get to the United States, but not through the sewers. William went to the American consulate in Tijuana to get permission to cross the border legally, and he was nervous. Tijuana was a center of cartel activity, and his passage to the United States was by no means assured. He could end up on the dangerous streets of this border city with no money. He went directly to immigration officials to present his proof of U.S. citizenship. All he had was the short version of his California birth certificate, a social security card with his number and some papers from the hospital in Los Angeles where he was born. He didn't speak English.

They grilled him for three hours in a windowless interrogation room where the air conditioning worked only sporadically. He was surrounded by stacks of papers, and he wondered whether these were evidence of rejected applicants. Finally, the officials left the room and said they'd be back with the verdict. William felt his entire future hung in the balance in this drab, bureaucratic room. The wait felt like an eternity.

The officials returned smiling and said that he could enter but advised him to get a long form of his birth certificate as soon as possible and a U.S. passport.

William had no money, no family in the United States. He only had a phone number of an old friend of his mother's, who he called collect. She had worked with his

Mom selling flowers in Guadalajara eighteen years before. She lived in Washington State and invited William to stay with her, and that's how he ended up in my classroom.

A New Home in Washington State

William's first reaction to the United States was culture shock. It really wasn't like the America on TV, nor was it like Guadalajara, William's home town. Further, although many people speak Spanish in his new small town America, it is nonetheless largely an English-speaking world. One of the first things William did was to enroll at the community college for English classes.

Next he set about looking for a job. However, the economy was at a low point. William had arrived in his new home just after the economic crash of 2008, and unemployment was very high. Many people were losing their jobs or were worried that they soon would.

He recalls, "No matter how bad the economy was in the United States, it was still far better than Mexico's. I landed a job at the Walmart bakery department. Early in the morning I'd bake bread, and at night, I'd go to English class. That was pretty much my life for a long time. My mother's friend and her family became my American family."

William began to appreciate his new community. In Mexico, he said, you can't trust the police or the government. Even though his family's business was so small, just a little tienda in their home selling milk, bread, and ice cream, the police would come by once a week and demand "protection money." William explained to me that the protection they needed was actually from them, the police.

"In Mexico, even for ordinary people, the cartels control everything. No one really even talks about it. It's just something you know. The government does nothing except try to collect more and more taxes, taxes heaped upon the protection money already demanded. There has already been social instability in Mexico. Students are protesting. Now it is much, much more difficult to cross the border into the United States, and Mexico's 'safety valve' of immigration north is almost gone. There is a large population of young, unemployed people with nowhere to go and little hope. "

William says the pressures are building in Mexico. "The drug culture and the gangs did not affect me directly, but it's clear that in the past few years, the plight of the poor is only getting worse. You cannot trust the thieves or the police, be they local or federales."

"Don't forget," he added, "Forty-three students were murdered in the State of Guerrero probably by the government. They were studying to be teachers, and I could easily have been in their group. If I had stayed in Mexico, I would have been attracted to their progressive program of study. The students were going to a commemoration of the 600 plus students massacred in 1968 when they themselves came under attack and were killed. I am reminded of the history I studied of life under President Diaz. In 1936, he raised taxes on everyone. There were taxes on windows, on dog food, on everything. That precipitated a revolution then, and we may not be that far from one now. "

Success!

Five years after William arrived in the United States with only partial documentation, penniless, with no friends or family in his new country and little to no English, he graduated with honors and a bachelor's degree from Western Washington University. His mother, father and twin sister came to witness this great event. William was not only the first person in his family to go to college and graduate, he and his sister were the first to even attend high school.

William's degree was in education with certification to teach in high school. As part of his training, he taught Spanish at a local high school. The students in his class were "legacy students," children of Mexican immigrants who "lacked confidence in both English and Spanish," William noticed. All could speak and understand Spanish, but William taught them to read and write what was, in most cases, their first language.

Cultural differences may account for some of the lack of confidence of these high school students. They have been raised by parents who are still very much products of Mexican culture, and they are very often from the poorest states in Mexico.

"In many ways these kids live between the Mexican and the American cultures. It took me awhile to adjust to American culture, and I doubt that I'm there yet. When you wait at a bus stop, even in small town Washington State, you don't really make eye contact with people. You are absorbed by your phone or your music, and you stay in your own bubble. People in Mexico have much more of a group consciousness. They are part of their families, their pueblos, and their neighborhoods."

The 'Macho' Latin Culture

William says, "I didn't learn about feminism until I came to the United States. The push for equality is a cool concept, and I hope that women in Mexico become more independent. Girls in pueblos are brought up in a very traditional way, but things are changing in the cities. You can't really equate how women are viewed in the United States with the role of women in Mexico."

"Yes, it is a 'macho' culture. However, you also have to remember what the Virgin of Guadalupe represents to us. She is a symbol ever present in our lives and is not even religious anymore. Or La Malinche who famously gave birth to the 'first Mexican' fathered by a conquistador, and she helped the Spanish conquer Mexico. You can only be 'macho' in relation to women. Women in Mexico understand that men will show their feelings, and they know they will be held in high regard. Part of being a man is being good to women."

It was obvious to me that William had been raised in a home where the women were held in high regard. William's idealization of women has not yet translated into finding an American girlfriend. "I think I'm too direct. Maybe I come on too strong, and I scare off the girls here. It's the Mexican way, and we don't even have a word for creep in Spanish, but that what I think American girls think I am."

"I had a serious girlfriend in high school. I asked her to marry me and come to the United States, but she didn't want to. Eventually she married someone else. The last time I was in Mexico, I met a nice girl. For me it was love at first sight. I was in Guadalajara for vacation, and I was walking back from my friend's house. We met on the street. We walked and talked, and I got her phone number. We texted and went out for the next two weeks. She's an accountant in Mexico, but she said she'd come to the U.S. as my fiancé. I don't know yet because I need a job and to get settled."

After Graduation, What?

Like all recent college grads, William went through a period of uncertainty. He moved to L.A. He and his sister had sponsored their mother and father, and the family, except for his step sister who married in Mexico, was together again for the first time in five years.

His parents had come north again reluctantly. His mother remembered her first try at living in L.A. and was nervous about coming back. But there is no work in Mexico for William's father, and he felt he had no choice. Before journeying north, this time with legal documentation, William's mother and father undertook a religious pilgrimage. They joined their priest and others and walked for days to a holy site. There they prayed to St. Toribo Romo Gonzalez, the patron saint of immigrants. People say that St. Toribo often appears to border crossers when they are most desperate. He is wearing a cowboy hat and boots and gives them water and money for their journey. Pilgrims come for miles and miles to pay tribute to the bones of St. Toribo.

William was determined to join his family in Los Angeles. Despite his years in the U.S., he still adhered to the

Mexican way of living with family, and he was a devoted son. He was undeniably changed by his years on his own at an American university, and he wasn't entirely comfortable being back under his parents' roof. He had trouble finding a teaching job and became involved with the Catholic Church in a search for answers to his questions. Perseverance finally paid off, and William found a job teaching in a charter high school in L.A. where I know he will be successful.

CHAPTER 3

DREAMER BEATRIZ

Field Girl
Little sparrow of the fields
Your open smile
And your joy
Are the brightest hope
Of a new day.

Alma Flor Ada

One summer quarter, Beatriz appeared in my classroom but not as an ESL student. She was enrolled in academic classes at the community college and wanted to volunteer. She was fully bilingual in Spanish and English, and she came from the same farmworker background as many of our students.

A natural teacher, Beatriz has confidence in front of the class and warmth and understanding in one-on-one teaching. When she offered to volunteer every night, I welcomed her to the class. Sharing a class with her was one of the highlights of my teaching career.

A Child Immigrant

Beatriz came to the United States when she was only eight years old. She was born in Campeche, Mexico, but her family moved to Tijuana when she was still little. Beatriz, her mom and her brother had tourist visas to come to the U.S. They worked in the fields and sent money to her dad. He came north eventually but with no visa. He walked across the border.

Every year in the United States, 65,000 undocumented students graduate from high school. They came to the United States with their parents when they were young. But who are they? The Wall Street Journal wrote: "We have long been fascinated by the cultural, linguistic, financial and other differences between first and second generation immigrants to America. They have been studied, written about, filmed…but how about the immigrants who came to this country with their parents? Are they first generation? They often speak English without the trace of an accent, attend public schools, dress, act, and look like American kids. And often they don't know they are here illegally."

The children of the 1.8 million migrant farmworkers in the United States often have a hard time in school. They move from school to school and even from state to state. In the season, they take time out to work in the fields. Many are below national averages in scholastic achievement, and the majority struggle to graduate from high school.

Beatriz is the exception. "I knew no English when I started public school in the United States. For four years, I was registered in an English as a second language (ESL) class. I was not allowed to speak English at home, so school was my only chance to learn and practice the language. There were only 15 Latinos in my high school, and all of us were enrolled in ESL. I had three friends from that class, but we had different lunch schedules. I was always a very shy person, and at lunch, I'd wander around with my tray looking for a place where I could eat. I wouldn't sit with the popular kids; that was out of the question. I'd sit at the end of the table where the smart kids were and not talk to anyone. They didn't speak to me either. It was traumatic and very lonely. I never thought about college. I just wanted to make it through high school."

Child Labor

Unlike most American kids, Beatriz worked from a very young age. When she was eight, her first job was watching her cousin's new baby.

"I got up at five in the morning and took care of the baby while my cousin worked in the fields. Sometimes I was scared to be alone, and I'd stay in the truck with the baby next to the fields. I did that for nearly three years."

After that, Beatriz worked with her parents on a farm. Her dad was the field boss and, from the age of 11, she did the same work as an adult.

"The worst part was working a machine that processed berries," Beatriz remembers. "It smelled of gasoline all day and burned berries. I worked from six in the morning to 10 or 11 at night, seven days a week. I picked berries, cucumbers, whatever. The only day I had off all summer was the day before school started. On that day, I would go to town and buy school supplies. That was my life until I graduated from high school."

At least forty percent of the children of migrant farmworkers also work in the fields. They, like many of their parents and others in their families, are often undocumented and, as such, are subject to the whims of employers.

Beatriz and her family had a good situation until one day they didn't. They lived on the farm where they worked. Everything was peaceful and productive. Then without warning, the owner of the farm changed the terms of their arrangement. He wanted more work for less pay. Beatriz' father is a very proud man, and he said they were leaving. He didn't know where they were going, but he wasn't going to stay at a place where he and his family were subject to the whims of a dishonest employer.

They were lucky.

"Some good American friends had a basement in a house down the road, and they said we could live there."

In a way, it was luck, but in another way, it showed the goodwill her family had built up in the community over the years.

"By then, my brother was married and had kids of his own, so it was just me and my parents. They took their life savings and started a small business, a taco truck, where they work seven days a week, 18 hours a day. We lived in that basement for a long, long time, and when the tenants moved out of the house next door, we moved in there. And there we still live."

Traditional Upbringing

The offspring who find themselves between generations follow many paths. Some rebel and have serious problems. Others, like Beatriz, perhaps because they have had to go to work when they were so young, and they take on a great deal of responsibility within the family, seem more mature than American-born children of their own ages.

Beatriz has thought about this a great deal.

"My parents have a lot of respect for me, and because I had so much responsibility, they trust me. When kids are expected to do nothing at home, they start to think that they deserve things. Kids here have opportunity, and I wonder why they don't always appreciate it. School is free, transportation to school is free, books are free, often lunch is free, and usually they don't even have to wear uniforms. So why do they go off and do bad things? It seems that maybe it's just too easy for them. They haven't had responsibility at home and haven't had to earn anything."

Responsibility and a strict upbringing that few American-born children experience explain a lot. When Beatriz' family went out, even to a family gathering, she and her brother were expected to sit next to their parents.

38

When they did something wrong, they were told right away not to do it again. They had no sodas, no junk food. Every day Beatriz' mom would pack her lunch, always Mexican food like a burrito wrapped in aluminum foil. Their only treat was an occasional weekend trip to Burger King. They ate very little meat but lots of beans, potatoes, eggs and rice.

"I was raised in a very traditional, very Mexican way. I wasn't allowed to go out without my older brother or father. I remember the first time I went to a party by myself, I think I was 21, and I thought the sky would fall in. It didn't, of course, but it didn't feel natural either."

Value of Education

If there is an unfair stereotype of immigrants from Mexico, it is that they don't value education. It is true that many arrive here with little or no formal schooling. However, the presence of my students in class, night after night, usually after a long day's work and family responsibilities, is testimony to their high regard for education. No one personifies this love of learning more than Beatriz.

"My family insisted on education. My brother and I were not allowed to go out. There were no drugs or alcohol in my family other than an occasional beer my father would drink at a party. We didn't have books at home, but I always knew that my parents valued education. All of my earnings went to my father, but he saved them for me. The money was there when I needed it."

Beatriz never considered going to college when she was in high school. At that time, undocumented students had to pay out-of-state tuition, and the expense was simply out of the question for Beatriz and her family, even at the community college. But then the State of Washington changed its law, and a counselor at the high school told Beatriz that she could now pay in-state tuition at the state universities and colleges since she had been a state resident for a long time.

"After learning that, I was nervous. I didn't know what classes to take to prepare for college. The counselor told me about scholarships for students who wanted to become teachers, and that was my life dream. I always wanted to be an educator. Scholarships paid for me to go to community college and then university."

Career Dream Thwarted

The lack of papers caught up with Beatriz. When she was a student at the University, she wanted to major in education and become a secondary-school teacher. The University's College of Education required a separate, additional application to ensure that all prospective teachers were legal, documented residents of the United States. It was a requirement that stopped Beatriz in her tracks. She still had no papers, and her dream of teaching seemed out of reach.

"I could attend the University, and I finished my bachelor's degree, but I couldn't pursue my dream to teach in public school. I really didn't know what to do."

In the United States, a common child-rearing practice is to encourage children to be independent and live on their own at a certain age. We bemoan 'boomerang' children who come home to live in our spare bedrooms and basements long after maturity. That's the way it started out for Beatriz.

Beatriz got married, and she and her husband lived in their own apartment for a year. Then her husband had to go back to Mexico for three or four months to help his family. His mother was very sick.

"When my husband left, I moved back in with my parents. I had a young son by then, and it was really good to be with them. When my husband was ready to return to the United States, we all went to California to help him. There was never really a question that my parents and my baby wouldn't go with me. I had a Washington State driver's license, but I had never driven anywhere except around my small rural town and my parents hadn't either, but we got into the car, and I drove all the way to California. We waited there a month for my husband to cross."

Beatriz's husband needed help crossing the border. It wasn't so easy by then. Since 2001, there are border patrols everywhere, and going through the desert can be a life threatening experience.

"Even worse is what can happen to you on the Mexican side of the border," Beatriz said. "After waiting so long and not knowing what was happening to him, I got a call that he and two other guys were beaten by Mexican soldiers at the border. They left him without ID, a phone, money, everything. He went to the police in Mexico, but they did nothing. They were used to these stories. Then a cousin took his picture, looking all beaten up and posted the photo on Facebook. The Mexican government shut down her

Facebook page. But by then, the pictures had been reposted and got around anyway."

Ultimately, Beatriz' father said he would pay a coyote $5,000, the going rate, to help her husband cross. He finally made it, and in celebration, they took their son, then a year old, to Disneyland. After that, Beatriz and her husband and son lived at home with her parents where they are to this day.

Beatriz stayed home with her young son and then continued at home when she had a second child, a daughter, who was born in November, 2012. She and many others watched the demise of the Dream Act in Congress with dismay. It would have given legal status to those like Beatriz who come to this country as young children.

DACA: A Reprieve

The Obama Administration became frustrated by Congressional inaction over the Dream Act. In lieu of legislative authorization, the Administration announced an executive action on June 15, 2012, that certain people who would have qualified under the now defunct Dream Act could get a two-year deferral from deportation or the threat of deportation, and they could get work permits. Known as the Deferred Action for Childhood Arrivals, DACA, the program set out an application process and eligibility requirements for people like Beatriz. These are young people who had come here as children and who completed high school or were now college students or in the military. More than 900,000 people were eligible to apply under what was quickly dubbed the 'dreamers' program. In the first six weeks of the program alone, the U.S. Citizenship and Immigration Services (USIS) approved 29,793 DACA applications or 99 percent of the total number of applicants during that period.

Beatriz' mother was quick to see the advantages of the new dreamers' program and urged her to apply. Beatriz' own daughter was only six months old, but Beatriz applied for the program soon after it was offered.

"I applied on a Saturday, and the following Monday I started looking for work."

From its inception through June 2013, more than half a million people had applied for DACA. Some seventy-two percent were approved, only one percent denied and the rest were pending.

The application process under DACA is not easy. You have to prove continuous residency and no criminal history, and the application fee is $465. About sixty percent of eligible applicants have applied, and about 75 percent of all applicants are from Mexico. Beatriz was so stressed by the process that she ended up in the hospital for two weeks. At the same time, her six month old baby girl was in the hospital with jaundice.

Shortly after Beatriz got out of the hospital, she was called for a job interview with the school system. At last her dream of working with children could come true, but going for a job interview was daunting and complicated for her. She'd never really had a true job. She'd always worked in the fields or with her parents on the taco truck. After that she was home with her own children for three years.

"I was very nervous although I thought I did okay at the interview. After I got the job, I found out that two of the applicants had Master's degrees, and two had experience as teachers. But I was the only one who was bilingual."

Beatriz came to her new job with the same qualities that she brought to my classroom as a volunteer. She understood, firsthand, the problems the students were facing both linguistically and in life. I felt privileged to give her a great recommendation. Although her work at the college in my class was voluntary, she treated it as a real job, and her contribution to the class was genuine indeed.

Beatriz now works as a teaching assistant and is going to the University for her Master's Degree in Education. She thinks of the United States as home and wants to make her future here. "I was back to Mexico two times since I left, once when I was 11 and then again when I was 15. Our tourist visas were still good then. I made my quinceanera (the traditional celebration of a girl's fifteenth birthday) in Mexico. My husband talks about returning to Mexico, but I want my kids to have the opportunity of a good education."

Uncertainty over the future of the DACA program bothers Beatriz, but she remains firm in her commitment to her dream. "Most importantly, I think I can contribute to society here. At first, the eighth graders I worked with were taking it personally that they had to go for language testing since English was not their first language. I could explain to them that the testing was to see how their language skills were evolving and wasn't punishment at all. They thought they were being tested because they were dumb. I could understand because that is what I had assumed too when I was in their situation. I am optimistic about the future."

CHAPTER 4

RITE OF PASSAGE FERNANDO

Stars or Flowers?
Are the stars shining flowers
That brighten the night sky?
Are the flowers drowsy stars
That lie sleeping in the fields?

Alma Flor Ada

Fernando works in the flower fields that cover some 1,000 acres of lush land. Every spring thousands of flowers bloom, and rows of yellow, white, red, and purple stretch out as far as the eye can see against a backdrop of snow covered mountains. The farm is owned by a family whose origins date back over 400 years of growing flowers.

For Fernando planting, shipping, picking and packing blubs and flowers are a rite of passage as much as it is a job. His journey north in 2009 was not an act of desperation as it was for so many of my students. For him, it was a challenge and an opportunity.

His life in Mexico was not that of a subsistence farmer. He was from the Guanajuato where he finished secundaria (middle school) and would have liked to continue on to high school, but there was no money for that. "I wanted to go, but the books, the transportation, the supplies and the tuition were more than my family could afford. I am the oldest of four children, and it just wasn't possible to send me to high school. "

"I worked in my family's small clothing store since I was 15. Then, I got a job in a grocery store as a cashier that paid $50 a week. I worked seven days a week, nine hours a day. It was probably all I could have hoped for in Mexico. I saw no real future, only survival. My father was already in California working. Our store didn't bring in enough income to support us. Without the money he sent home, we would have gone under."

To the North

"When my father returned from America, I decided it was my turn. Until he came back, I felt I had to stay and help my mother. I was 19. I wanted to see what life was like north of the border. I didn't know what to expect except that I would work. Work was the one certainty."

Fernando is an example of how Mexico has steadily been losing its young, its best and brightest, and its hardest working to the rich country in the north. The American

Dream is not just for Mexico's poorest, subsistence farmers. The trip north also appeals to young men and women from all walks of life who want to try for a different future.

"In communities with a long tradition of migratory activity, migration may become a 'rite of passage' for men coming of age...Sending communities lose young men during their most productive years as laborers...in sending communities, '(i)t is common for the young people with the most initiative to leave.'"

Fernando certainly seems representative of young people searching for a new life and experiences.

"I didn't leave Mexico because there was something wrong with my life which was great in many ways. Every night after work my friends and I would go out. We would walk around the town, listen to music, hang out at the coffee shops around the zocalo. On holidays, we'd go to the hot springs that are only about 15 minutes from my house. There, for $9, we could spend the whole day. There were rides, food, and, of course, hot springs. I cannot say I was leaving a bad life. It wasn't bad. It just had no future."

Guanajuato is famous throughout Mexico and indeed throughout North America because of the annual pilgrimage to the top of Cerro del Cubilete mountain, the geographical center of the country. There, more than a half a century ago, a lone pilgrim ventured to the mountain top in search of a miracle because doctors told him he was dying. Now he is more than 80 years old, and he still makes the trip to Cristo Rey by horseback. More than 4,000 riders join him every year. They pray near a more than 65-foot tall depiction of Christ the King which stands at the top of the mountain. People leave notes there asking for their own personal miracles.

"I went there myself before coming to America," Fernando tells me. "It gave me strength and faith to make the trip. I thought it would be difficult, and it was to a certain extent. But I felt the way was paved for me by my pilgrimage to Cristo Rey."

Crossing the Border

Fernando paid a coyote $900 to help him cross from Senoyta, Mexico, to Arizona.

"We didn't stand a chance on that first attempt. Immigration chased us with helicopters and four wheel drive vehicles. We weren't mistreated, just apprehended and sent back. The immigration officials called it 'catch and release' as if we were undersized fish. I waited awhile before I tried again. I waited until it felt right to me."

Fernando's second attempt was successful. It was February when the desert is not as punishingly hot as it can be later in the year. He was with the same coyote because for the $900 fee, he was given a second try. And again, immigration chased them, but this time, everyone scattered.

"I found myself with my cousins who were also trying to cross. I don't remember being afraid. In my mind, it was more like a challenge, or even a game. We were on one side of tall bushes, and immigration was on the other side. I don't know how we were not apprehended again, but we weren't."

Finally, they were near a freeway. They could see a McDonalds on the other side of the highway where the green and white Border Patrol vehicles were parked.

"We ran into another group of Mexicans trying to cross over and tried to link up with them, but they were afraid of us at first. Since my cousins and I are fair skinned and blue eyed, they thought we were U.S. immigration officials. The helicopters were circling, probably looking for us. At last they moved on, and we took our chances and ran across the road dividing us from the United States. We aimed for a place as far from the MacDonald's as we could. We could hardly believe our luck. We made it, and no one was coming after us, and there were no helicopters or barking dogs. It was quiet, and we were free!"

Out of Arizona

Nearly half of all illegal border crossings from Mexico to the United States are into Arizona where many are apprehended. An average of 1,374 crossers a day were stopped from 2001 to 2010. Fernando and his cousins came through in 2009, a year before the Arizona State legislature passed the toughest anti-immigration measure in the country. Known as Arizona SB1070, it allowed law enforcement wide latitude in stopping and detaining anyone suspected of being in the country without papers. Parts of the law were eventually struck down by the U.S. Supreme Court.

"Even before that law, we were afraid of Arizona, and tried to make it out of there as quickly as possible. We had very little money, but we were lucky and caught a ride going north. We didn't even really know where we were going, just out of Arizona. I was very, very lucky to end up in Washington State."

Fernando's first job in the United States was inspecting eggs. Poultry farming, chicken processing and egg production are all big business in the region. After about a year, Fernando got a job in the flower fields, and he was still there when he enrolled in my class.

"I work from 7 am to 6:00 at night, seven days a week. After work, I go to English class four nights a week. My goal is to finish my high school diploma, and continue at the college to be certified in welding."

Fernando has cousins who live nearby, and it was at one of his cousin's wedding that he met his own bride.

"Maybe it was love at first sight," he recalls. "I saw her from across the room, and I liked the way she looked. I wanted to get to know her. It was a traditional Mexican wedding in that men mostly talk to other men and women to women. Every once in a while I could get a glimpse of her. She was always surrounded by friends, and they were laughing and smiling. I think she looked my way once or twice. It's possible she saw me looking at her."

"At last the ceremonies and the eating were over, and the music began. I made my move and asked her to dance. She smiled at me. After our dance, I asked her out. We started going to movies, to the mall, out to eat. She's an American citizen, but that is not why I love her."

Fernando married her just two years after their meeting at his cousin's wedding.

Being married to an American citizen does not guarantee you the right to stay in the United States. If you did not enter the country with a visa, then the prospects of being allowed to stay are not good. You are not safe from deportation, and you have no papers to work legally in the United States. Comprehensive immigration reform probably would have provided relief for people like Fernando, but it failed to pass in Congress.

In the absence of reform, President Obama issued an executive order which would have allowed those married to U.S. citizens and who are essential to their well-being temporary relief from the threat of deportation and granted them papers to work legally. It was modeled after the DACA program that provides some protection to young people who arrived in the country before they were 15. This executive order was challenged in court and, as of April, 2016, its fate is pending before the Supreme Court. The Court agreed to hear the case, but it is a divided Court. In June of 2016 in a 4-4 deadlocked decision, the Court sent the case – the United States v. Texas -- back to a lower court where President Obama's executive action probably will languish.

Without this executive order, people like Fernando who marry Americans are required to return to their country of origin and wait their turn to immigrate legally. This can take 10 years or more until your name comes to the top of the list. Most, like Fernando, choose to take their chances here rather than leave their families for long periods of time.

Under the Obama Administration's executive order, husbands or wives of citizens would only have had to return to their home countries for a brief stay before legal readmission. While they await judicial action, people like Fernando live in limbo.

America Is Now Home

For Fernando, America now feels like home. He and his wife have a daughter, and he spends every possible minute with them.

"I love to take my family to the beach even though the water is way too cold for swimming. And last winter, we went to the mountains, and I saw snow and glaciers for the first time. We have nothing like that in Mexico. You can play in the snow year round here. My daughter and I spent hours making angels in the snow. I felt so free and happy."

"I want to raise my daughter here. Even though it's true that we have to protect our children so much, and they can't just go out and play in the streets the way I did, it is still a better way of life. In Mexico, things have also changed. There are criminals now and soldiers and police who are like criminals. It wasn't like that when I was growing up. Now the cartels control so much and people are afraid of being caught in the cross fire. There are even rumors of children being kidnapped and held for ransom or worse. Probably the children must stay inside more there now too. "

"My future is here. I only hope that the American government will find a way so I can be here without fear of deportation. I want to finish high school, even attend college, and my daughter can have a good education and whatever future she chooses. For me, I came in search of fun and work, but really it is the American dream that holds me."

CHAPTER 5

THE OVERSTAYER ROSA

Bird

Little bird flying over the fields,
Where do you take the dreams
I place on your wings?

Alma Flor Ada

Rosa was born in Trujillo, Peru, called the "capital of everlasting spring," the country's second most populous metropolitan area. It's located in northwestern Peru near the mouth of the Pacific Ocean. In 1966, her family moved to Lima to pursue greater economic opportunities, and Rosa finished high school there.

A Carefree Childhood in Peru

"I had lots of friends, and we had a great time. We were always going to the movies, drinking coffee at cafes, running to dances and parties. We didn't even need to make appointments to see each other and go out. Somehow we just came together to enjoy life." Rosa loved high school and had a circle of friends she's kept in contact with her whole life. They laughed and shared stories of school, boyfriends, clothes, all typical of coming-of-age. "It was a carefree life full of dreams and possibilities."

Then life changed for Rosa and her family and many other middle class people in Peru. Rosa's family were jewelers. "My parents worked in gold and silver, and we became targets for criminals, and we were scared. My parents were robbed at gunpoint three times. We thought the next time they might not be so lucky. The first time, the gunman demanded money. The second time, they tied up my mother and father and threatened them if they didn't pay 'protection' money. And the third time, they beat up my father even though he had paid because they wanted more." Rosa's idyllic life with her friends in Lima came to an abrupt halt

It was a dangerous time in Peru. Shining Path, Peru's Maoist communist group was very active in Lima and are considered terrorists. They set off bombs killing innocent civilians. They disrupted power supplies and people never knew when they'd have electricity. They assassinated business and political leaders. They demanded money from the city's many small businesses like Rosa's family. By 1991, Shining Path controlled a large part of Peru's countryside and had a sizeable presence inside and outside of Lima. The organization never had the support of the majority of the people, but still it made life there uncertain, dangerous, and very difficult.

Shining Path's activities caused upheaval in the lives of ordinary Peruvians. Many had long gravitated to the United States but before the 1980s, most immigrants from Peru came to find greater economic opportunities. They were working or middle class Peruvians looking to better themselves. But in decade of the 1980s, the demographics changed and many in higher income brackets left the country fleeing Shining Path. By 1992, the number of Peruvians in the U.S. shot up to about 500,000 from about 200,000 in the mid 1980s.

Shining Path's war against "bourgeois democracy" drove people like Rosa and her family out of the country. At the beginning, the group tried to lead a "People's War" to overthrow what they termed "bourgeois democracy." But Shining Path soon financed its operations by growing and smuggling coca, the raw ingredient for cocaine. It wasn't long before their cause for poor peasants became instead a campaign of violence and brutality against the very people they were supposedly helping. With the capture of the organization's leader in 1992, the group's influence has steadily declined but continues to exist in skeletal form mainly because of drug revenue. Much of the country's illegal drugs are produced in an area known as the VRAE (Valle de los Rios Apurimac, Eneymantaro) in southern Peru where Shining Path still controls a small territory.

Any Port in the Storm

Rosa set off for Switzerland. "It was never intended as a permanent destination, but I felt like I was running for my life. By that time, I had an infant son from a very brief marriage to my high school sweetheart. We were both 18, and the marriage didn't stand a chance. I left my young son in Peru with my parents while I went abroad to make money to support him."

Rosa worked as a housekeeper in Switzerland. The money was pretty good and it was a relief to be out of Peru. "I had fun in Switzerland. After the tensions of life in Peru, it was a great. My parents had to close their jewelry business and the money I sent home helped them prepare to leave the country too. My work paid well, and I had a little money to travel in Europe. The work wasn't difficult, but I missed my family, especially my son and my parents, and I knew that I didn't want to be a housekeeper forever."

A Tourist Visa to the U.S.

Rosa was lucky. She secured a tourist visa to the United States in 1990 and never looked back. Her immediate family was already in America, and she joined them in Miami. Nearly 20 percent of ex-pat Peruvian community lives in Florida with the remainder concentrated in California (16 percent), New Jersey (16 percent), and New York (12 percent).

"I felt that I had to leave Miami or I would never learn English. Spanish is everywhere there, and you can go from morning to night, day to day, week to week without ever really needing English. I knew that I wanted to continue my education and, to do that, I had to have English."

The 'Overstayer'

To know Rosa, the term "illegal immigrant" does not come to mind. After all, she is Peruvian and did not simply cross our southern border. She arrived in the country by air with only a tourist visa and didn't leave when the visa expired. The term is 'overstayer,' and it is estimated that about 40 percent of the people in the United States without documentation are people who arrived with tourist or student or temporary work visas and simply stayed or "overstayed" their visas.

It was (and still is) possible for overstayers to obtain documentation or legal status by marrying an American citizen. This is just what Rosa did.

"It was before the internet with all of its sites to match up people. I met my husband through 'Love Mail,' a matching service coordinated by a church in Florida. We had a nice relationship, but we just aren't the same. He wanted to travel, and I wanted to stay in one place, continue my education, and raise my son. I left, and he stayed in Florida. I wanted to go to Canada, but Washington State is as close as I got because I couldn't get papers for Canada. We divorced, but remain friends to this day, some 20 years later."

At first Rosa studied English. Once she was away from Miami, it was apparent that Spanish alone would not suffice. Although there are quite a number of immigrants from Latin America in western Washington State, most people speak English. She worked as a housekeeper by day and attended class at night. Rosa made rapid progress through the English as a second language (ESL) levels and within a fairly short period of time, was ready for regular classes at the community college.

Rita was not one of my students. By the time I met her, she was attending community college and her English was more than passable. I met Rosa because we both sold goods at fairs. She sold jewelry that her brother would make and send to her from Lima. He was the only close relative who hadn't come to the United States. I sold goods that I designed and had made in Bali, Indonesia. We were 'vendadoras' together, and I always enjoyed it when we were at the same markets. When I started teaching ESL I needed someone who was fluent in English and Spanish, and I asked Rosa to be my teaching assistant. She helped me in class for over a year.

A Single Mom

Rosa moved rapidly from ESL to teaching assistant to student at the community college, an immigrant success story. At first she studied office technology because she thought it would be a ticket to a job that paid pretty well. But life intervened, and she had to take time off her studies to support her son and her niece who had come to live with her. Raising children in the United States is not easy, Rosa soon found out.

Her son's education faltered. His high school was not a good place for him. Even though he spoke Spanish fluently, he was not Mexican, the dominant Latino group in the community. He ran into trouble and Rose thought, "I have lost him. I came all this way to lose my son. I had doubts about coming to America. I came for my son, and now he was in trouble."

Life in American high schools is not easy for anyone. For Latinos in Washington State, it is fraught with many dangers. I have had more than one young student in my classes of high school age who didn't want to go to high school. One 18-year old student told me, "Teacher, I can't go back there (to the local high school) because everyone I know there is a criminal. I want an education, and I want English. My father will kill me if I go the way of my high school friends." He graduated from community college.

As difficult as it was to be an immigrant in the United States, it was about this time when Peruvians in the United States had a reminder of how difficult and violent life could be in their home country. On December 17, 1996, the embassy of the Japanese ambassador to Peru was raided by the Marxist group known as Tupac Amaru Revolutionary Movement (MRTA), a close cousin of FARC. Hundreds of high-level diplomats, government and military officers who had been attending a birthday celebration at the Ambassador's home for Emperor Akihito were taken hostage.

It was a very dramatic time indeed. The MRTA resented Peru's close ties to Japan and didn't like Alberto Fujimori, Peru's President at the time who was of Japanese descent. Throughout the coming weeks, which stretched into months, President Fujimori pretended to negotiate with the Maoist group. In secret, he was planning to take the Ambassador's house and free the hostages. His operation was largely held to be a success although one hostage, two commandos, and all the MRTA members were killed.

Overcoming Obstacles

Rosa thanked her lucky stars that she was no longer in Lima. Things eventually turned around for her and her son. He attended the community college and graduated from Central Washington University. He now lives and works in Patterson, New Jersey, considered by many to be the center of Peruvian life in the United States.

Rosa herself returned to school and finished her associate's degree at the community college while working full time helping new moms and their babies get a good start in life. She went on to the university to get her undergraduate degree in social work. Along the way, there were major obstacles. The biggest was her health. She was diagnosed with a very serious and life threatening form of cancer. Her son flew back from the east coast to help her.

"Even during the darkest hours of chemotherapy," Rosa recalls, "the university was my salvation. From six to ten at night, four nights a week, I went to class. Even though it was a half hour's drive from my house, I persevered. My father taught me that persistence is the way to get what you want. He passed away in my house but lives on as a voice in my head. He cheers me and supports me on my journey."

Now Rosa is planning to go back to the university, this time to get her Master's Degree in Social Work. She wants to be a counselor in the latino community. Rosa has been back to Peru but doesn't regret leaving. "I've been back to visit my brother who still lives in Lima and my friends there. Many of them have done well." Peru's economy is no longer in the deep trouble it was in the 1980s or even the 1990s. In fact, in some ways, it's fared better than the U.S.

economy since the economic collapse in 2008 which didn't really touch Peru. The country's economy grew by 9.8 percent in 2008, and 6.3 percent in 2012. "The culture still seems wonderful to me. It is spontaneous and joyous. Now that the country is doing better, people are able to live more fully."

Affirming the American Dream

Rosa has lived on the financial cliff since her arrival in Miami all those years ago. She struggled to raise her son, and then her niece, and to cope with her parents' aging and her own illness. Through it all, her outlook affirms the American dream. "Here I discovered education. I firmly believe that education is what makes the difference in a person's life. No one can take that from me."

Rosa continues to make a difference in the lives of low income families. Sometimes I have accompanied her on visits to moms who were my students. She brings diapers, love, compassion, and help to mothers struggling to care for their babies in a new world.

She doesn't regret leaving her home country. "Peru's economy is better but life there still has a dark side. The very problems that gave rise to Shining Path and other extremist groups persist today. For many in Peru, when I lived there as now, the economic boom might as well be on a different planet."

Today Rosa owns her house and enjoys a circle of good friends. She received her master's degree and continues to serve the community. She has been cancer free for five years.

CHAPTER 6
A LOVE STORY MARIA AND MARTIN

Love

How good it is to love our friends;
How easy to love our grandparents;
And the finest blossom of all,
The love we give our parents,
Our brothers and our sisters.

Alma Flor Ada

Many seek romantic love, but it is not easy to find. Maria and Martin's story unfolds like a movie. If you believe in fate, then you may find that some things are just meant to be. I think you will understand.

Meet Maria

"Come in, come in," urged Maria.

I was welcomed like visiting royalty, told to sit in the dining room while Maria finished up in the kitchen. I was there to interview her, but there's no such thing as a visit to Maria's house without food.

I felt, somehow, I was stepping back in time into my Grandma Minnie's kitchen. Grandma Minnie, an immigrant herself, presided over a very small kitchen out of which the most amazing meals would emerge. Although Maria was not like my grandmother in most obvious ways, they are both centers of energy in the home and definitely in charge of their kitchens. In my Grandma's apartment, the kitchen was about three or four feet wide and maybe five feet long. If there was counter space, I don't remember it. As children, we would gather around a table in an adjoining eating area. The table was protected with a clear plastic cover in anticipation of messy, delicious food that would grace the table. It was much the same in Maria's house.

I chatted with her from the dining area as she made tortillas in the kitchen. She blended masa with a flower from the cactus plant and with fresh cilantro and spinach leaves. My mouth was watering as she effortlessly put the mixture to fry in the tortilla pan and then served the tortillas with a salmon soup made from fish she and her husband had caught themselves. I didn't think I was hungry, but when presented with such a feast, I couldn't resist.

Maria had only recently arrived from Puerto Vallarta, Mexico, and was a student in my beginning English class.

Maria's Story

"I was born in a very small pueblo in the mountains of the State of Jalisco. La Estancia de Landeros has less than 200 residents. My parents worked with wood and made soap. We were extremely poor, and there was no school nearby, not even a primary school. I went to live with my mother's parents when I was 6. When I finished primary school, I had to move again since there was no middle school where my grandparents lived."

"When I was 14, I went to take care of my aunt, who had just had a baby. In those days, women had someone to care for them for 40 days after childbirth. That was my job. I did the washing, the cooking and the cleaning. I also made tortillas every morning. When I was in the kitchen, I couldn't help but see a handsome boy watching me. He sat on the garden wall and stared at me. I have to tell you that it made me nervous. I decided to do my chores earlier in the day to avoid him."

"One morning as I was cleaning the kitchen, I looked up to see the boy running from the yard. Then I saw a rock with a paper wrapped around it."

Martin's Story

"Boys in Mexico have the run of the place. We are not protected the way girls are in the villages. My job was to feed the horses where the new girl was staying. I'd make a point of going over there early to watch her in the kitchen. She looked happy making tortillas and preparing the meals.

I wanted to meet her, so I wrote a note. The outside of the letter said, 'Open this letter, and you'll find my heart.' Inside was a piece of paper folded into a heart shape. My message was 'I'm sorry if I am bothering you, but I so much want to meet you. I hope we can introduce ourselves to each other. I have a feeling that you are the girl I've been waiting for all my life.'"

Martin said he really didn't know what to expect. Girls that young weren't allowed to talk to boys, especially strange boys.

"She was new in town, and I wanted to be the first to meet her and talk to her. I waited the next day outside the house where she was staying. After awhile, she came out and started walking to town. I asked her if we could sit down for a minute. She said she was going to the store for embroidery thread. I asked her name, and she said, 'Maria,' but she said she couldn't stay long because she was afraid that her aunt would see us and get upset."

Maria Moves Away

When Maria's aunt was stronger, it was time for Maria to move away to go to middle school. She went to Las Tancia and attended a private middle school there. It was expensive, and to help pay her way, she made and sold tortillas and tacos at soccer games. She was embarrassed to be a vendor there because the players were her same age, and some might recognize her.

Maria moved to Puerto Vallerta for high school.

"I remembered Martin even long after I moved away. He was my first love, my first crush. Every time I would think about his heart-shaped note, I would blush. After high school, I took a job working for two women doctors. One of the doctor's husband tried to rape me. I told my boss, but she didn't believe me. I realized, then, that if I wanted to be protected, I needed to get married. I was 21 years old, and it was time.

"I don't remember ever loving my husband. We were married for 19 years and had three children. He wasn't a mean man, and he didn't beat me. But I wasn't happy, and I didn't want to be married to him anymore."

Her parents didn't approve of divorce. They thought that if he wasn't hitting her, she should stay married. When her parents left for a visit to the United States, Maria decided to get a divorce while they were away. By the time they returned, it would be done. Maria had a small store that supported her and her children. It was then 2002, and Maria was 40 years old.

Maria was so happy to be free of her husband that she would sing everyday in her store. People would gather around to sing with her. Her children were happy, and life went on without serious problems.

Martin Goes North

Martin moved away shortly after he sent his love note over the wall. He was studying in Baja, California, preparing to be an accountant. He ran short of money part way through his studies and decided to join his brother in the United States. His goal was to work for a year, save money and return to finish his schooling. He never went back.

"It wasn't that easy to get into the United States," Martin recalls. "Even though it was only the early 1980s when it was much easier to cross, immigration sent me back to Mexico three times. Finally, I made it and went to Wyoming to join my brother. Later, I moved to the Pacific Northwest where I have another brother."

Once Martin started working in America, he saw that there was another way to live, another way to make a living.

"My eyes were opened. In Mexico, if you have a fruit tree, the government wants all the fruit. And what the government doesn't take, the cartels will. In the United States, you just plant more fruit trees. Sure the government will take some, but there's plenty left for you."

Martin got married in 1985. He has two children from that marriage. He was divorced in 2002, the same year that Maria left her husband. Martin works as a supervisor at a large factory that makes artificial crab meat. He qualified for documentation under the Reagan Administration's amnesty program and is an American citizen.

Maria and Martin Are Introduced

Maria's nephew, Felipe, got married in Puerto Vallarta.

"My wife and I have the perfect match for you," Maria's nephew kept telling her. "He's a single dad and lives in the United States. I know you are meant for each other. He's my wife's uncle."

At the same time, Martin's niece kept phoning him about a wonderful women who would be perfect for him.

When at last, he decided to return to Puerto Vallarta for his mother's 91st birthday celebration, his niece arranged for him to meet Maria at a restaurant.

She went to the restaurant and, although over 20 years had passed since she had last seen him, she knew right away it was him. He was the boy who sent her the note in the garden. Martin didn't recognize her.

"I didn't have a clue," he said.

They talked about their lives. They laughed about how they had both gotten married at about the same time and divorced the same year. They shared how their sons had the same name and how his daughter was named Maria too.

"You don't remember, do you, about the papelito (little paper)?" Maria finally asked him. She then recounted the story of how he'd thrown the rock and the paper over the garden wall all those years ago. She told him how she went into the yard and found the rock. When she opened the note, "my heart opened too." Maria was too young to date, and she needed to finish her education. She left the village without speaking to him again.

"As she talked, I felt like I was watching an old movie. It all came back to me. But there were lots of other girls I chased, and Maria was from such a traditional family that she wouldn't talk to me. I thought she was too difficult, so I forgot about her and went on with my life. Don't forget," Martin reminded me, "I was older than her and ready to move away. But then I remembered everything. I remembered tossing the note over the wall and waiting for

70

a chance to speak to her. I loved watching her make tortillas in the morning."

After their blind date, Martin went fishing with his buddies in Mexico, and he didn't attempt to contact Maria again. But she wasn't about to let go of who she thought of as her first love. She called him in the U.S. to see how his fishing trip had gone. The more they talked, the more they realized how much they had in common. Seven years had passed since each of them divorced. Two of Maria's children had married and left home. Only Manuel, then 12, was still at home. Martin's younger child, a daughter, had returned home with a grandchild.

Each phone call brought them closer. They shared, and they laughed when finally, Martin asked Maria, "What is our next step? Would you come to the United States? And what would you do if it doesn't work out?"

Maria told him that yes, she would come, and if it didn't work out, she'd just go back to Mexico. Martin was elated because that was the right answer. She was an independent woman, and he could be free to love her. He didn't have to worry about a new immigrant wife. He booked a ticket to Mexico.

Before he left, he bought a ring. He said it was the cheapest engagement ring he could find. After all, it might not work out, and it would be better not to spend too much on a ring, he told himself.

The Proposal

The families gathered for a huge party. Martin's family and Maria's family were all there. Food was brought out, one dish after another, followed by music and dancing. It was a great fiesta. Martin asked the musicians to stop for a moment, and he asked everyone to be quiet. Then he took Maria by the hand, and led her to the center of the room. Martin got down on one knee. There wasn't a sound in the room. Everyone had stopped breathing. Martin took the cheap ring out of his pocket and asked Maria to marry him. She never noticed that the diamond was so small. She was just happy that her very first love would be her love again.

Martin returned to the United States and applied for a fiancé visa for Maria. Maria went to Juarez to the American consulate for an interview. No one could doubt that this was a real marriage, filled with love and promise. Their application was approved, and five months after the proposal, Maria and her son flew to the United States.

Some 36,000 people entered the United States on fiancé visas in 2013, the last year for which data are available. Lately, there has been some controversy over this type of visa, know as a K-1 visa, because one of the shooters in the San Bernadino, California, terrorist attack in 2015 entered the U.S. to be married to the other shooter. Most of the concern, however, about the fiance visa has been over whether or not the marriage is a 'sham' arranged to give someone access to the United States, usually for economic reasons.

In Maria and Martin's case, the marriage took place within a short time after her arrival in the country. They have now been married for three years. Maria was determined to learn English and was a joyful presence in my class.

CHAPTER 7
THE AFFLUENT IMMIGRANT JORGE

One

Not one flower but many,
Each with a different fragrance
Not one fruit but many,
Each with a different flavor.
Not one tree but
A hundred different shades of green!
All together
on this planet.

Alma Flor Ada

From the first moment I met him, I knew Jorge was different from the vast majority of the ESL students at the college. To begin with, he had completed three years of a university advanced technology degree in Mexico. His interests were different from other students. For his birthday, he treated himself to a Cirque de Soleil show. He said he'd wanted to see them perform live for a long time. I share his love of Cirque de Soleil, and I wanted to interview him to find out more about him.

"There's something you should know about me," Jorge told me at the very beginning of our interview. "It may change how you see me, but I need to tell you. I am gay." I told him it was just not something I had thought about, and it really didn't matter to me, but it was clear that it was very important to Jorge and a central part of his story.

He continued, "For as long as I can remember, I've felt different. I was born in what is called a rancho community, a suburb about three hours from the Texas border. It was a new subdivision, and my class was the first one to attend our primary school, a one-room school with grades kindergarten to six. We shared a teacher. Primary school wasn't too bad, but by middle school, everything changed, and not for the better."

"For one thing, I didn't wear the same clothes as the other students. They all dressed in cowboy gear, cowboy boots, jeans, and white cowboy hats. I didn't like those clothes. I didn't ride a horse and, in fact, I had no interest in horses. I wore black everyday. I guess it was punk. I had three friends in middle school, two girls and a boy, and we all dressed in black and tried to look as different from our cowboy cohorts as we could."

Jorge was bullied for being different in middle school. "People always wanted to fight me. They called me 'gay' and, although I was beginning to realize that this description might be true, I was nowhere ready to admit it. One student wanted to be nice to me and offered to have a fake fight. He'd pretend I had punched him in the face, and then the bullying would be over. But I told him no, I didn't want to fake anything."

Jorge told his parents what was happening at school, and that he wanted to change schools, but they said he couldn't. They said he needed to face his problems and deal with them. Jorge struggled through middle school and thought it would never end. "Whenever I could I would pretend to be sick. I knew I had to go to school, but I tried to avoid it as much as possible. I am the first of three boys in my family, and no one else seemed to have the problems I did. So I hung out with the few friends I had and tried my best to live long enough to get to high school."

Acceptance at Last: High School

"No one from my middle school went on to high school, called prepatoria (or prepa for short) in Mexico," Jorge was relieved to report. This is fairly typical of Mexico where less than half of students continue to finish high school. By high school age, many if not most are expected to contribute to family income and, only the well off, and highly motivated continue in their education. Although public high schools are nominally free, students must buy their books, provide their transportation, pay for lunch and uniforms and all supplies. Many high schools are private, tuition-charging institutions.

"My high school was in Saltillo City, about 45 minutes from my home. For the first two years, I took the bus. Then my father gave me a 2006 Toyota to drive to school. My family is fairly well to do. My father owns an automobile repair shop, but he has also other businesses and real estate. I am among a lucky few."

At last, Jorge felt accepted. He made good friends, and he did well in high school. He studied hard and got good grades. The student body was large and diverse and there was no more bullying and no more cowboy dress. At last, he could go to school without worrying whether he'd be beaten up.

"But the biggest change happened when I joined the Ballet Folklorico," Jorge tells me. The Ballet Folklorico is Mexico's celebration of traditional dance and costumes. Jorge threw himself into the ballet. "Then my life and my heart soared. I felt truly alive. When I was on stage, I remember feeling happy, really deeply happy, for the very first time in my life. Hearing the audience applaud erased all the suffering I had endured."

"It wasn't just on stage that I felt good. I was surrounded by people who accepted me for who I was. I didn't need to wear a cowboy hat or pretend to be macho. I could be myself."

Problems Return

Jorge's father didn't approve of the Ballet Folklorico. "If an activity didn't pay, then it wasn't worth doing in his book. Also, I would have to come home late from practices and performances, and my family thought that it was dangerous. Maybe it was." Jorge quit the Ballet because "it just wasn't worth going against my family. Nothing is more important to me than my family. Not ballet. Not anything. My grandmother thought that ballet was for gay people. I hadn't told her yet that I was gay."

By the time Jorge quit the Ballet, he'd been in the university for a year. He continued on with his studies for another two years. He majored in robotics engineering, a field in which his father thought he could make a living. Jorge was a solid B student, not outstanding but certainly respectable.

Leaving the Ballet began a whole series of problems for Jorge. He broke up with his first boyfriend. Eventually he dropped out of the university, and his parents didn't speak to him for a week. He still had not told his parents that he was gay. "When I was in the Ballet, I could just be myself. My life was satisfying and happy. I didn't need to talk about my sexuality." But his ex-boyfriend wanted to get back together. He stalked Jorge, following him, showing up where he knew Jorge would be. If Jorge wouldn't get back together, the boyfriend threatened to reveal to his parents his sexual orientation.

Rather than wait for them to hear about his homosexuality from a stranger, Jorge decided to tell his family himself. It was a Sunday, the day the family was together to eat breakfast and catch up on the week. He asked everyone to come into the living room. He had something important to tell them. He told them about his ex-boyfriend and the threats. He told them everything. After he had poured out his heart, the whole family, his mother, father, three brothers and his grandparents stood up together and left the room. "I felt like I was a bad person. No one would speak to me for weeks. For a long time, the only one who spoke to me was my grandfather. Later, my family came to accept me for who I am. They surrounded me, hugged me, and told me they loved me no matter what. I felt such relief."

"But even with their acceptance, I wasn't coping. I dropped out of university. I fell deeper and deeper into depression. I started hanging out in clubs. I was drinking a lot. Sometimes I was so drunk I didn't know where I was, and I couldn't find my car."

"I still lived in my family's house, but I was like a ghost there. I drifted through the night, lost and wandering through the city. This was dangerous, but I was beyond caring. Homophobia is very real in Mexico. At times I was threatened, and I thought I might be attacked. It's pretty common for gays to be murdered, even in Mexico City, but more commonly in smaller cities like where I was. One night I came close to serious harm. Fortunately, a policeman helped me. That's somewhat unusual in Mexico where the police aren't always on your side."

Redemption

"My descent into hell lasted an entire year. I'm not even sure what my family thought. They watched in horror, helpless. I even contemplated suicide, almost unheard of in Mexico," Jorge recalls.

"Change began when I started going to church. There, everything turned around. A priest invited me to a three day retreat. A small group of us went off to a cabin away from everything. We didn't have electricity, running water, or any modern convenience. Of course, cell phones and computers were not allowed. It was a complete retreat from the modern world."

What was to Jorge a retreat was an everyday reality for many of my students. More than a few of them grew up without any trace of modernity, without even electricity, or running water, or school for that matter. Jorge was privileged and comparatively rich. He had been able to attend school, even high school and university, goals that were beyond the reach of most of the students who attended my English classes. Yet Jorge had to withdraw from the privileges he's been born into in order to find himself.

The Catholic Church dominates in Mexico. Although there has been separation of church and state for a long, long time, the Church tends to have authority in issues of morality. The new Catholic Catechism describes homosexual acts as "grave depravity," but it also says that homosexuals "must be accepted with respect, compassion and sensitivity." However, they should be steered towards a life of chastity.

"After the retreat, I spent a lot of time talking to the priest. I also went to a psychologist who helped me accept myself. I think my parents thought that the psychologist could turn me into a normal person; that is, not gay, but it doesn't work that way. I talked with the priest about my sexuality. The Catholic Church doesn't accept gay people, but the priest told me that it didn't matter that I was gay. The Church accepted me and just wanted me to be a good person. That was a turning point for me."

Discrimination in the Workplace

Jorge looked for a job. His depression lifted and he was ready to engage with life again. He had a high school diploma, three years of university engineering training and a diploma from a technical school as well. This background put him way beyond the typical applicant in Mexico's job market. However, he didn't know English which was important even in Mexico because so much business is international.

"I ran smack into discrimination. One prospective employer even asked me if I was gay. In Mexico City, discrimination based on sexual orientation is against the law. Although same sex couples have even been able to marry there since 2010, and after 2015, in the rest of the country, outside of the capitol there's a lot of prejudice against gays. It's engrained in the culture."

Mexico's national soccer team, El Tri, was fined $20,000 by the Mexican Soccer Federation for anti-gay chants that came to characterize their games, even during the World Cup. Now, "in one of the first campaigns of its kind, El Tri players are speaking out against their own fans over the use of the anti-gay chants." The team even began an anti-discrimination initiative, dubbed *Abrazadospor el Futbol*, or 'Let's Embrace for Football,' to encourage fans to have more inclusive outlooks.

Notwithstanding legal or public relations efforts, discrimination persists, especially in the workplace. Jorge couldn't find a decent job and he decided to look north. Unlike many of my students, he didn't have to run across the desert in the middle of the night. He applied for, and got, a ten-year, multiple-entry tourist visa showing the difference that money can make.

The Flight North

His family thought that moving to the United States was not something to be done lightly. His father first went to visit an aunt in Florida, Jorge's first choice of a destination. The aunt was ok, but his father discovered that her sons were 'chollos', bad guys, dealing drugs and heading towards serious trouble. So Florida was out.

Jorge's father then went to visit another relative living in Arkansas. But there too the dark side had claimed another son who was doing time in prison. A third option was San Antonio but Jorge said no. He wanted to get away from home to begin again, and Texas was too close.

Finally, his father visited an aunt and uncle living in Washington. This aunt was clever and showed her brother only the good things about life in there. It was a small town with little crime. There were jobs. Spanish was spoken almost everywhere. Jorge's father said ok to Washington State, and never even noticed that in this relative's family too, the son stayed home all day smoking pot.

Jorge left Mexico on July 15, 2013. "In many ways, it was the only way I could leave home," he explained. "It's uncommon for Mexicans to move out of the family home without a good reason, like a job in another city or marriage."

He arrived determined to learn English. "I noticed that Asian immigrants made it a point to learn English before they did anything else. I decided to do the same." Jorge showed up in my beginning ESL class. He attended every evening, and progressed rapidly. He placed into an advanced English class, and is now studying at the college level.

"Even though I live in small town America where homosexuality is not totally accepted, I feel a sense of relief. In Mexico, violence against gays is common, and in my state, Coahilla, although same sex unions were legalized in 2007, attacks on gays continue. I realize now that I never felt safe."

In fact, a survey of gays in Mexico reveals that almost all of them feel there is discrimination against them, and many suffer from mental illness as a result. From 2002 to 2007, according to the Chamber of Deputies of the Mexican legislature, 1,000 people were murdered in Mexico in homophobic crimes. Mexico has the second highest rate of homophobic crimes in the world (after Brazil). The most frequent problem, however, is not violent crime but discrimination in the workplace. It is hard for a homosexual to get a job in Mexico which had definitely been Jorge's experience.

What's Next?

Because Jorge entered the country legally on a tourist visa, he has some options that are not available to those who enter without documentation. When the U.S. Supreme Court legalized gay marriage and required all states to recognize same sex unions, it opened the way for gays and lesbians to gain a green card in the U.S. through marriage. Marriage, either heterosexual or homosexual, to U.S.

citizens and permanent residents enables spouses to be eligible for green cards.

Jorge is contemplating this route to making his stay in the United States more permanent. He wants to live here, complete his university education here, and work here.

The marriage option, either heterosexual or homosexual, is not available under most circumstances to those who entered the United States without papers. But for Jorge, who came with a valid Mexican passport and a tourist visa entitling him to be in the country legally, marriage is a time-tested option now made available regardless of sexual orientation. All he needs to do is fall in love with the right partner.

For the Wealthy: Another Option

It has not gone unnoticed in Jorge's family that his life in the United States is better, freer and presents many more opportunities. Life in Jorge's home state of Coahuila, Mexico, is fraught with difficulties.

The U.S. Department of State warns U.S. citizens to defer all nonessential travel to Coahuilla. Violence along the State's highways presents continuing security concerns, and high rates of murder, kidnapping and armed carjacking persist. For everyone, especially the wealthy who are targets of kidnappers for ransom money, the threat of violence has become a daily concern.

The region encompassing Coahuilla has been described as a massive grave site. Human rights groups put the number of 'disappeared' at close to 200,000, although the Mexican government puts it at 26,121.

Time magazine ran an article in January, 2013, describing an "exodus of Mexican migrants fearing for their lives and battling corrupt officials for business interests." One category of migrants from Mexico, the wealthy, has been growing while overall, migration from Mexico to the United States is at net zero or, by some measures, actually declining. One way wealthy immigrants can legally enter and stay in the U.S. is the EB-5 Investor Program.

"My family is considering the EB-5 investor route," Jorge tells me. "My father sees greater opportunities in this country. His motivation is also because of his sons. One of my brothers had been attending high school in Texas but, after he went home to Mexico for the holidays, he was denied reentry to the U.S.

Under EB-5, investors need to spend between $500,000 and $1,000,000 on investment projects in the United States and create at least 10 jobs in the process. They are then eligible to apply for up to 10 legal resident cards for themselves and unmarried family members under the age of 21. At 24, Jorge would not benefit, even if his father choses this route to legal status.

The EB-5 program, established in the 1990 Immigration Act, has recently come under criticism for fraud and abuse. It was extended under the Omnibus Spending Bill passed by Congress in December, 2015. Presumably, the extension gives Congress time to evaluate the program and make changes if it decides to extend it again. It will also give Jorge's family time to decide about participaton.

Different and Wonderful

Every weekend Jorge volunteers at the local Opportunity Council to help the elderly go shopping, do chores around the house, and he keeps them company. Like flowers, fruits, and trees, people come in many different forms.

"Yes," Jorge says, "maybe I am different from most people, but after much suffering, thought and reflection, I know that the most important thing to me is to be a good person." When you are with him, you know you are in the presence of someone wonderful.

CHAPTER 8

AMNESTY'S CHILD CARMEN

Pride
Proud of my family
Proud of my language
Proud of my culture
Proud of my people
Proud of being who I am.

Alma Flor Ada

In my mind's eye, I see Carmen crossing the border. She was, in her words, "a skinny kid who liked to play outside." She was 12 years old. Her father put her in a coffin, in the back of a pickup truck. The coffin was small, only big enough for a child or a very small adult.

"Be quiet," her father told her. "Say nothing until you see me again. Play dead."

"I was so scared. I couldn't breathe. I was under a pile of sweaters and clothes. I thought I really would die. All I wanted was to get out of there. I wanted to yell to my dad, but I knew he couldn't hear me. He was riding in the front of the truck. It felt like forever. My mind went back to my first communion. There I was, a little girl in a big church expected to act grown up. I felt the same in the back of that truck," Carmen remembers. "I think I passed out or fell asleep. I heard someone speaking in English, and I thought it was immigration. I didn't move until I heard my dad's voice. He said, 'It's ok, darling. You can get out of there.' I was so happy. I was alive and I was in America."

An Undocumented Teenager

Thirteen years old, Carmen was already an 'alien' without papers, brought to the United States to take care of her nieces and nephews. She'd left her childhood, the rest of her family, and her familiar pueblo back in Oaxaca, Mexico. Her pueblo was small with only about 390 people living there, only 28 of whom had jobs. Carmen and her mother, sisters, and brothers waited for money sent home from the north, money from her father. By 2000, some 20 percent of the people in Oaxaca had left for other parts of Mexico or the United States. Many more have left since then.

Going north for families like Carmen's was an economic necessity, not a choice.

"Even though dad sent us money, we were still very poor. Mom made hats from palma (palm tree leaves). The money she made from selling hats went to buying flowers that you boil. They make a crunchy sound when you eat them, and they taste good. My sister and I sold the boiled flowers. Sometimes the man who bought my mother's hats didn't give her money. He paid her in fruit, and us kids would fight over the fruit."

Carmen knows that they were very poor, but she also remembers the feeling of belonging in her pueblo, the feeling of being free where you live.

"I have a family of three sisters and three brothers. Yes, we had nothing. Our floor was dirt. But we were happy because we were always with family, and everyone in the pueblo knew us. We had many friends, and we could go anywhere we wanted. We were too poor to buy uniforms for school, but we were allowed to wear our own clean clothes. Shoes were the worst. Mine were plastic, and they always fell apart."

In Carmen's memory, everyone was poor. In fact, seventy-five percent of Oaxacans live in extreme poverty. Many don't learn Spanish until they go to primary school. She explained, "My first language is Mixteco. I learned Spanish in school. We still speak Mixteco at home. I had to leave school after sixth grade to move north. I had to help my family."

Life in the United States

"I thought I could go to school in the United States but my mother said I didn't need to," Carmen remembered. "I asked her why, and she said "because you're a girl, and only boys need to go to school."

88

For three years, Carmen took care of her nieces and nephews so her brother and sister-in-law could work in the fields.

"When I was 15, my dad 'fixed' my papers to make my age 21. But I was so skinny that the field bosses didn't believe it. I don't know how my dad convinced them to let me work, but he did. That day I was in the fields picking strawberries."

Carmen remembers how she felt. "It was a bad day. At 6 a.m. my mom put a hat on me to cover my face and a sweater. By afternoon, the sun was out, and it was hot. I didn't need the sweater. They gave me a little cart with two boxes. One was for the good strawberries and the other for juice strawberries. Around 3 in the afternoon, it started to rain. I didn't have boots, only tennis shoes. Since I didn't have a raincoat, my mom put a garbage bag on me fitting it over my head like a pancho. The cart kept getting stuck in the mud. My first day at work, and my whole body was in pain."

In the United States, over 1.8 million people work as seasonal farmworkers, and many are children like Carmen. Farmworkers earn an average of $7,500 a year, well below the poverty line. Like Carmen and her family, most are migrant workers who travel from place to place depending on the crops.

Legal Documentation for Carmen

"When I was 16, my dad got me papers for real. I'm proud of him for doing that. He got papers himself under the amnesty program for farmworkers. I don't know how he did it. It was expensive to get documents for the family, but after that, I was a legal worker."

Carmen's father qualified under President Reagan's amnesty program, which gave documents to some people working in the country without papers. He was eligible to apply for his family to get status as well.

Carmen now had documentation to work legally in the country but, other than that, not much changed. She still worked on the farms picking strawberries, blueberries, apples, lettuce and grapes. She travelled from California to Washington State, up and down the I-5 corridor wherever there was work.

"I still did the same work, but I felt more confident. I knew I could go back to Mexico and visit my family and return to the United States to work again. When I turned 20, I got married. We went to Mexico to get married. I don't know why I wanted to get married there, but I just did. We had a traditional Mexican wedding in my pueblo. I was only sad that my mother and father were not there because they couldn't afford to travel. We stayed in Oaxaca for two weeks, and then we came back to the U.S."

When Carmen and her husband returned from Mexico, life was the same as before. They travelled the same path as her parents.

"We went from farm to farm, state to state, crop to crop, always working."

The Most Terrible Day

Carmen and her husband were working on a farm in Washington State. By then, they had two children and lived in migrant housing on the farm.

"We lived there for the season. One day I was picking berries, and I didn't know it was the last day I would see my mom. We were working together in the fields. It was almost the end of the day. My mom was really thirsty, and she asked for water, but I only had juice. She drank the juice."

After work, Carmen went back to her cabin, and her mom went to her apartment in a town not far away. Carmen decided to take a rest before taking a shower. Everyone always showered after working in the fields. It was important to wash off the pesticides. She knew there would be a long line at the showers, and the hot water would be gone quickly.

No sooner did she lie down than someone came to her door.

"Carmen," he yelled. "Carmen come quickly. You have to come. Your mother had an accident."

"You know, when you hear the word accident, you imagine something is broken. I never imagined anything so terrible. I saw the car right away. A car and a pickup truck. It was my cousin's car. I recognized the car. Everything was smashed. The ambulance wasn't there yet."

Someone told Carmen that her cousin was driving. Her cousin's baby was in the back seat crying, and her cousin ran the stop sign. These are rural farm-to-market roads, and people drive fast on them. They had a piece of wood in the car. It was shaped like a triangle and was used to clean blueberries. The wood hit her mom's head.

"She had a blood clot on her mind," Carmen says. "My mother was 42 years old. Her name was Amanda."

A helicopter arrived and took Carmen's cousin and her baby to a hospital in Seattle. It was too late for her mom. She died at the scene of the accident.

The story was that her mom was heading back to the farm to find out about her paycheck. It was a Friday, pay day. Even though Carmen's mother couldn't read, she knew that the check was wrong. She had only been paid the minimum hourly wage, not the amount per pound for all the berries she had picked. She was on her way to the office to talk to someone about her check.

After her mother's death, everything changed for Carmen. "I thought, why does this happen. Why do we have to work so hard and this happens? Is this why we came to the United States? I know we have to work hard, but do we have to do this?"

Carmen's mother also left a five-year-old daughter behind.

"My dad left for Mexico right after the accident. He left for another woman, another life. I don't know how he thought his children were growing up. After my mom died, he changed his life, and he forgot about us. I already had two kids of my own. My sisters and my brother raised my youngest sister. She went to school. She's now 17, and she finished high school. She's a good person even if my mom's not here."

America: Land of Education

Carmen decided that the reason she was in America was to go to school. In Oaxaca, people only go to school on average for seven years. For Carmen, it was even less. She signed up for night-school English classes. She is intelligent and dedicated and attended class four nights a week, two and a half hours a class. It is a big commitment for people who work all day and have families to care for as well.

"After my Mom passed away, my husband and I wanted to stay in one place and not follow the jobs from farm to farm, state to state. My son was sick too much. The cabins at the farm were damp and cold, even in summer. And the air from the farm had pesticides. The doctor said moving all the time was bad for my son. We rented an apartment, and we've been here ever since."

Carmen and her husband have permanent resident documents, but even with legal papers, life is not easy. She took a job in a factory. The work was dangerous, and the people were not always nice. She continued to come to class and was a very good student. But her education was cut short once again when her family needed her in Mexico. Her grandmother was sick, and there was no one to care for her. Carmen went to Oaxaca to help her grandmother, putting her family and their needs before her own.

When she returned, the factory laid her off. She applied for unemployment compensation. This was Carmen's opportunity to go to school during the daytime. It was her dream to become a nurse, and the first step would be to qualify as a Certified Nursing Assistant or CNA.

A New Career

"Going to school to become a nursing assistant was really hard for me. I only had a sixth-grade education in Mexico, and my English wasn't that good. And the classes were not like ESL classes. I did homework until two every morning. Sometimes I cannot imagine what the book is talking about. But I finished, and I passed my State tests. Now I work at a long-term care facility," Carmen says with evident pride.

Carmen likes to work with the elderly. She is kind and loving, and she genuinely cares about them.

"Many old people here are all alone. It makes me very sad. As caregivers, we are like their family. We comb their hair. We do their nails. We help them take a shower. What you think about doing for yourself, you do for them. Many times, they have no visitors. And sometimes, they don't know what they are doing. They are forgotten people. I try extra hard for them. It's different from Mexico. In my country, we take care of our old people. They are not so alone."

Carmen is a hard worker and doesn't usually complain. She is proud that she finished the CNA program and wants to work in her chosen field. Still, she is surprised by the conditions at the long-term care facility, where there is only one caregiver for every 12 residents. Caregivers are expected to do everything: the laundry, housekeeping, serving meals, feeding people, cleaning up, doing the dishes, everything. And sometimes the residents are difficult. They kick; they punch; they insult the caregivers.

"It's not really their fault," Carmen explains. "It's part of their condition. But we feel bad anyway. We try our best. Sometimes I come home, and I am just sad."

The Immigrants' Dream: A Better Life for Their Children

Recently, Carmen went back to Oaxaca to care for another aging relative. This time it was her grandmother on her father's side. She took her daughter with her. She told me that things seem better there now, probably because people are sending money back from America, but still there aren't any jobs.

"Because of money from America, more children are going to school. Everyone seemed to have enough food. People have shoes. Houses are fixed up a little. But I didn't see very many people working. There are no jobs for us. Not in my State, Oaxaca. How can I tell my children to study hard and become a doctor if there are no jobs for doctors? They will just have to go back to the United States and work on farms like I did. I cannot imagine that I can live in my pueblo again."

"I stay in the United States because I want a better life for my children. My kids are good kids. They know what my husband and I have been through. They don't want to live like we did."

For Mexican parents of American-born and raised children, there are many worries. Carmen knows this all too well.

"Some kids change in America. Maybe their parents are from Mexico. They work hard and try to do their best. But their kids are American kids, and it's hard to talk to them sometimes. We are from two different worlds. They don't always want to listen. They can be rude. At night in my apartment complex, I often hear people screaming at each other. Once in awhile, there's violence. It's scary. There are drugs and gangs and many problems in the world that our kids have to face."

To Oaxaca: I See for Myself

So many of my students are from Oaxaca that I wanted to go there and see for myself what it was like. I arrive in Oaxaca City, the State's capitol. The weather is perfect. It is December, almost Christmas, and I don't need a sweater during the day. The sky is a wonderful bright blue, and only 'vacation clouds' float by.

At night, the whole city is in the zocalo (city square). There's food for sale. Musicians are playing in the center of the park on a stage. Folklorico dancers attract a crowd on a different stage. There's a big manger scene where families wait in line to visit the baby Jesus. Red poinsettias line the square. Images of Our Lady of Guadalupe are everywhere. Cafes face the zocalo, and people pass the time by drinking coffee, talking, eating, and watching other people. Everyone told me to come for the Night of the Radishes, Oaxaca's famed celebration of Christmas with carved radishes. Carvers make nativity scenes and animals out of radishes that are especially grown for the event. They can be up to 20 inches long and weigh over six pounds. The Night of the Radishes is December 23rd, and I decide to come back for that event.

To be in Oaxaca in December is fantastic. I take local buses to visit archeological sites. I go to the weekly markets, a different one for each day of the week. At each market, people are there selling everything from vegetables, mounds of fried grasshoppers and crafts to ordinary household items. There were live animals, and everywhere there is wonderful food. At one market stall, a cook, busy at work, is the twin image of Frida Kahlo, the famed Mexican painter who died in 1954. I stop at her stall for lunch, and I don't take my eyes off of Frida's double.

But where are the crowds? Where are the people shopping for the week? The roads to the markets are not busy. The buses have plenty of empty seats. Have most left for America? I think of all my students who travel from remote villages in Oaxaca to make a living in the United States. Their ghosts are everywhere. Mothers spread their goods at the markets, but their faces are long, unsmiling. Their sons and daughters are gone and may never return. How many of the children of Oaxaca, I wonder, would love to come back if only they could find work?

CHAPTER 9

REMITTANCE MAN EDUARDO

Honor

Honor is the work

We do in the fields.

Honor is the family

Who loves and cares for one another.

Honor is being true to myself

As I wake up each morning.

Alma Flor Ada

Eduardo entered the ESL program in the Spring quarter of 2014 as a beginning English learner. The college administers a standardized test to all entering students, and the students are tested again at the end of the term. Eduardo tested level 6 in reading and listening to English, the highest level of the ESL program at the college. Why he was placed in my beginning English class I don't know.

In some ways, Eduardo was like many of our students. He worked in the fields, and he was from the Mexican State of Oaxaca. But he was different in important ways too. He was older than most people in the class, probably in his fifties. Also, he was from Oaxaca City, not a small pueblo far from an urban center. Sometimes, he said things that were more like poetry than broken English, and he carried himself with what I can only call a sense of honor, of knowing who he was and where he was going. I was curious and wanted to know more about him.

Beginnings

Eduardo was born in Oaxaca City. Tour books describe Oaxaca City as 'fortunate" in that it sits in a temperate highland valley at 5,110 feet above sea level, and enjoys a year-round temperate climate even though it lies far south. The origins of Oaxaca derive from the Zapotec people, Eduardo's ancestors. They settled in Monte Alban on a mountaintop above what is now Oaxaca City. Visitors today see the ruins of Monte Alban where rulers lived for over a thousand years.

Eduardo's family still spoke Zapoteco when he was a child, and they were proud that two of Mexico greatest leaders, Benito Juarez and Porfirio Diaz, were Zapotec from Oaxaca. Eduardo's family soon fell on hard times. When Eduardo was three and his sister one and a half, his father left the family and went to live with another woman in another state. His mother couldn't support Eduardo and his sister. She brought them to live with her mother in a small pueblo a couple of hours from the city. She went away to take a job, and send money to her mother.

Eduardo missed his mother, but life was pretty good with his *abuelita* (grandmother). They lived in what would be called extreme poverty. There was no electricity, no running water, and the floor they slept on was dirt. Many in Mexico, and especially Oaxaca, live in poverty. Over 12 percent of the State's population has no electricity. Almost 30 percent live without running water. And some 27 percent have dirt floors. In all, nearly three-quarters of Oaxaca State's 3.4 million residents are poor.

Eduardo had the run of the village. He and his friends played all day long and went home for meals and 'abuela love.' He remembers being happy and enjoyed the freedom that is probably true for children in villages around the world. Everyone knows you, and you know everyone. You belong there. You know the places where you can play, and you live your young life without worries. You don't have much, but then no one else does either. Eduardo's life went on like that for two years.

Grief

One terrible day his grandmother died. He came home from playing to find her on the floor, and saw that she wasn't moving. He cried, "Abuela, abuela. Wake up. Wake up." But she didn't. He ran next door to get the neighbors. His sister was sitting next to their grandmother crying. The neighbors came running over. Eduardo picked up his sister. There was no warning, just one day when everything changed. The neighbors were nice, but they had their own children, their own problems. They were too poor to take in more little children. Everyone in the pueblo came together to bury his grandmother. Eduardo tried not to cry, but he couldn't stop himself. He and his sister cried and cried. No one in the pueblo knew how to contact Eduardo's mother.

Eduardo told me that his grandmother died from exposure to the smoke from an indoor cook stove. She would get up each morning, and make a fire to cook the tortillas for the day. Millions die each year because of the indoor air pollution caused by these stoves, from pneumonia, respiratory illness and cancer. Eduardo's grandmother was one of them.

The day after the funeral, Eduardo took his sister by the hand, and they walked down the long hill from their village to the main road. It was hot and dusty. They were alone and hungry. Without food, without money, they waited hand in hand for the bus to come.

"Where are you going?" The bus driver asked. "Oaxaca City," Eduardo answered. "We don't have any money. We are going to find my father's family." The driver let them get on the bus. They were, after all, children five and three years old. To Eduardo, even years later, it didn't seem unusual for two young children to be travelling alone without an adult. A lady gave them a few tortillas with a little cheese. Someone else gave them some fruit. After a while, a man got on the bus and started playing his guitar. For a few moments, Eduardo and his little sister forgot their troubles.

A Future Filled with Problems

"Oaxaca City," the driver called out. Eduardo took his sister's hand, and they got off the bus. In truth, he didn't really know where he was going. All he remembered was a green house in the City. That's where his father's family lived. He didn't know where his mother was. Somehow, and to this day he doesn't really know how, he found the house. He found his father's parents and sisters. He found the green house. He was so happy. He didn't realize that his problems were just beginning.

His father's family called Eduardo's mother, and she came as soon as she could. She was working in a village about three hours away. She knew that something was wrong. Her husband's family would take care of her daughter, but not Eduardo as they didn't think he was really their son's child. Eduardo's mother took him to what he described as a "government boarding school." His mother had no money, no husband, and no family left to help her. She had no choice. She didn't want Eduardo to see her crying so she tried to smile and told him to be brave. She would be back for him as soon as she could. Eduardo could see the tears falling down her face, and he cried too, not loud crying, but the soft, quiet tears of a broken heart.

In reality, Eduardo was in an orphanage. Like so many children who end up in orphanages around the world, he wasn't really an orphan. He had a father who had left him. He had his father's family who didn't want him. And he had a mother who couldn't afford to take care of him. Even today when parents are absent or dead or too poor or sick to take care of them, children like Eduardo enter a world without family and the world of child labor.

"My life changed in boarding school. I went from being a carefree kid in my grandmother's pueblo to being like a little soldier. There was a time for breakfast, lunch and dinner; a time to get up and sleep; a time to shower; and, a time to go out and earn money for the school. "

For all of his first five years, Eduardo was loved, and he shared that love with his little sister. All of a sudden, he was alone in a strange new world, a world where the beds were all lined up in a large room. It was a world with long tables and not enough food. It was a world where the adults had all the power and no love to share.

Eduardo made a decision. He knew he was only five years old, only a boy. But in his mind, he decided to do his best. He would be brave for his mother and wait for her to come and get him. In one way, Eduardo was lucky. His orphanage provided education, and he wanted desperately to learn. In the pueblo, he had fallen in love with a little girl. Even as a small boy, he was a romantic. She had bright eyes that smiled at him and black hair that curled down her back. He wanted to read and write so he could send her letters. He learned fast and started writing letters. And, although he never received a reply, he continued to love the girl in the pueblo.

Life in the Orphanage

Life in the orphanage was not easy. There were bullies who took his books, his pens and the little money he made shining shoes in the zocalo (city square). The bullies got away with violence. Usually the bullies were older students at the orphanage, but sometimes they were the teachers or the people who ran the school. He says, "Some were nice, but others were not." And then a look crossed his face, and I knew that he had suffered at the orphanage, suffered at the hands of older, bigger kids and of adults who were cruel and abusive.

"Every time you stepped out of line, someone would hit you," Eduardo recalls. "Even sometimes when you had done nothing wrong, someone would hit you. It was a way of life for a long, long time."

Sundays were a day off at the orphanage. In the mornings, they would go to church. Eduardo liked church. He liked the smell of incense, the music and the polished benches. But the afternoons were what he liked best. For children like Eduardo, who had no visitors, Sunday afternoons were free time. They were allowed to go to the zoo which was near where they lived.

One Sunday, Eduardo remembers, he and his friends were walking to the zoo when, all of a sudden, everyone was running towards them, away from the zoo entrance. Then they saw why. The lions had escaped from their cages and were chasing the people. Eduardo and his friends understood the situation and started running too. They ran as fast and as far as they could, and climbed trees to wait for the police and firemen to catch the lions and return them to their cages.

Eduardo was at the orphanage for seven years. For the first year, he would hear from his mother every few months. She wrote to him of her love for him. She missed him, and couldn't wait until they could be together again. Then there were long periods of time, years, when there was no word from his mother. Eduardo was lonely for his mother. Even in silence, he remembers thinking that his suffering was her suffering, and he waited for her return.

"One day when I was 12," Eduardo tells me with tears in his eyes, "I saw a woman in the hall talking to the school's director. She looked familiar, but I didn't recognize her at first. The director waved his hand for me to come over. Then I saw. It was my mother."

They hugged each other until there were no more hugs left. He knew that one day she would come for him, but it was still a big surprise when he saw her. She said she was a nurse now and had a job at a hospital in the city. They would have a home, and his sister would come to live with them also. For all these years, his little sister was living with their aunts, their father's sisters. Eduardo had not seen anyone in his family since that day when he left the green house for the orphanage.

Eduardo was happy for the first time since he was five years old. He was with his mother and his sister in their little house. Eduardo went to school, not just a school in the orphanage but a real school, a middle school. Eduardo worked hard, and he was a good student. Other kids would invite him to their houses. He saw that they lived differently. They had enough food, nice clothes and even toys. Eduardo was smart, so the other kids would get him to do their homework. They would give him clothes and food.

School in Mexico was supposedly free. Secundaria (middle school) in Oaxaca City was tuition free, but students had to buy their uniforms, lunch, transportation, books and school supplies. Even with his mother's salary from the hospital and food and clothes from his friends, Eduardo couldn't afford school, and he left after 10th grade.

He wanted to go to work to help his mother. He didn't want to lose her and his sister again.

While living at the orphanage, he sold goods in the zocalo (or town plaza), sometimes woven bracelets or flowers. Or he would shine shoes when he got a little older. Now he needed a real job. He went to work in a store that sold fertilizer and other things to farmers. He made 25 pesos a week or about $2. The work was ok, but it wasn't enough money to help his mother and to keep his sister in school.

"Life in Oaxaca is very hard," Eduardo explained, "even for an adult worker. I couldn't make much money." At least 75,000 children in the State have to work to survive on their own or to help their families.

Life in the Army

As soon as he was old enough, Eduardo joined the army. He was stationed in Acapulco, far from home. It was his first real job, and, for the first time in his life, he knew where his next meal was coming from. He had a roof over his head, and he had money to send to his mother to keep his sister in school.

Eduardo was alone and lonely. "I didn't want a career in the military. In the army, corruption is everywhere. It wasn't for me. After three years, I left the army and went back to Oaxaca. I missed my mother and my sister. For a brief time, I was married. It didn't last long, but now I had a daughter. My wife left me and my little girl."

Back in Oaxaca City

"There weren't many opportunities for me there but at last, I got lucky. I got a job working for an American artist who made bronze statues in Oaxaca. I loved the work. I loved feeling something beautiful coming from the metal. The artist finished his work and went back to the United States. I didn't know what to do next. Now I needed to help my mother, my sister and my daughter."

There is no social safety net in Oaxaca. There is no unemployment insurance or workers' compensation, no food stamps or welfare and no food bank for that matter. As a grown man, Eduardo knew he had to help his family. The only real safety valve for Mexico's economy is that it shares a border with the richest country in the world. When there is nothing else to do, you go north.

For most of our history as neighbors, migrating from Mexico to the United States was not difficult. In 1985, Eduardo simply decided to go to Los Angeles with a friend who was making the trip. He easily joined the sea of Latinos moving north to America. From Oaxaca alone, net migration is over half a million, and by the year 2000, some 662,000 people left the State of Oaxaca for another part of Mexico or the United States.

In all, about 20 percent of the State's population has left. "The money they send home becomes crucial to the survival of the towns they leave behind." In 2006, Mexicans working in the U.S. sent $25 billion home. In pueblos and cities throughout the country, children wear shoes to school because of these remittances. Houses are built and repaired and expanded. Businesses are started. Fields are planted.

For many years, remittances have kept a 'lid' on things in Mexico, especially in the poorer states like Oaxaca.

Life in Los Angeles

Eduardo worked in a drycleaners in L.A. "I had my California driver's license. I paid taxes, and I sent money home. I was an honest worker. One day I found a solid gold coin in a jacket left for dry cleaning. At first I thought, 'keep it.' But then, I decided to do the right thing, and I gave the coin to my supervisor. Today he owns the dry cleaning shop, and I am once again an undocumented worker in the United States."

Eduardo lived in the United States when President Reagan's amnesty program, adopted under the Immigration and Control Act of 1986, gave many undocumented workers and their families papers. Eduardo was not eligible to apply. Only people living in the country since 1982 or before or people who worked on farms could apply. Eduardo wasn't worried because then, it was easy to cross the border and get a job. He thought he could return when he needed to.

Return to Mexico

Eduardo recalls, "I would have stayed in Los Angeles, but my mother was sick. She almost died. I lost her for so many years when I was a child, and I was afraid of losing her again perhaps for good. So I went back to Oaxaca City. The money I sent to my mother was used to support my sister and my daughter, and to start a little store in our house. It wasn't much, but after a while, I bought game machines for the store. We became popular in the neighborhood for our electronic games. In all, we had 11 game machines."

"I was in Oaxaca when everything happened. We took to the streets. The teachers asked for more money. A teacher in Oaxaca earns about $220 every two weeks. They have to use that money to buy chalk, pencils, and other supplies for the children. They went on strike, and we supported them. The year was 2006."

People lived on the streets, and they refused to leave. They were tired of being neglected and lied to by the government. They marched through Oaxaca City and called for the Governor to resign. Eduardo remembers, "I was excited. I marched with the protestors. I was also afraid. An American journalist, Brad Will, was shot and killed during a demonstration."

After six months, the government moved to stop the strike in May 2006. Twenty-six Oaxacans had lost their lives during the protests, and many more were arrested and jailed. "But we took to the streets again! And this time, 300,000 people marched. It was violent, and many people were put in jail."

After so many years of broken promises and terrible poverty, the people of Oaxaca had had enough. They had some success. In 2010, a new governor was elected, Gabino Cue, a former mayor of Oaxaca City, who promised real change.

"I stayed in Oaxaca after the protests because I wanted to be with my daughter. I wanted to see her grow up and finish high school. Every day I watched her grow from a cute little girl into a beautiful young woman."

"It was just me, my daughter and my mother. We all lived together in the little house with a store. My daughter was my life and I didn't want to leave again until she was 18. My father had left me, and I couldn't do the same to my own child. My sister lived nearby with her husband and child. It was a happy life."

North Again: More Difficult, More Dangerous

"When my daughter graduated from high school and was engaged to be married, I decided it was time to return to the United States. I needed to make more money. Some things were better in Oaxaca. Our government was better, but still there were no opportunities for me. To get ahead, have some savings, and maybe start a business someday, I had to leave again."

Only this time, it would be different. For one thing, Eduardo was older. Now he was 52. After September 11, 2001, it was much more difficult and dangerous to cross the border. Eduardo was crossing in 2013 and the border was a very unfriendly place.

The United States and Mexico share a 1,954 mile border. Since 2001, the number of border patrol agents doubled. Now, there are more than 18,500 agents. There are fences, cameras, lighting, walls, drones, and surveillances systems all along the border. It is almost impossible to cross at the old, safer places near cities. Instead, crossers are forced into the Sonora desert where there are fewer patrols. These areas are far more dangerous because of the heat, especially in the summer, the snakes, and the confusing terrain.

Some people pay coyotes or guides to get them through the desert. Eduardo didn't want to pay a coyote, and he didn't have enough money. He knew that these guides often left people in the desert to die. At the first sign of trouble, they ran off, leaving the crossers alone in a hot and difficult desert. Since the mid-1990s, the remains of more than 6,000 people have been found in these borderlands. Eduardo did not want to be one of those who died of thirst, exposure or snakebites trying to get to the United States.

"It took all my army training to cross the border. I was dressed as a bicyclist in tight pants and shirt. I had a pretty nice bike which I carefully lifted over one wall and then another. I was technically across the border. However, I saw the Border Patrol off to one side not far away. I rode furiously and then hid my bike in the bushes. I got down into the bushes. But I wasn't alone. There was a rattlesnake there too. I was more scared of the snake than the Border Patrol. Somehow I escaped both. Finally, I got to a 7-11 type store, went in and bought a pastry and drink, and called a friend in San Diego. My friend came and picked me up. My second chance in America had begun."

In Search of a Job

Eduardo started out again in Los Angeles. He has friends and family there, people to stay with, people who care about him. It was comfortable.

"However," Eduardo says, "You can live your life there and never have to speak English. The Latino community is huge, but it was the middle of the recession, and there was a lot of competition for jobs."

111

"I went further north to Washington State to look for work. My nephew was already there. I found a job on a farm, and went to English class at the local community college."

Eduardo sends money home every month. He helps his mom, and he sends special money for his dog, a schnauzer named Feroz. "Her name means 'fierce' in English but she's anything but fierce. She's a kind, gentle pet who was my daughter's constant companion," Eduardo explains. "Now, with the money I send back, Feroz can eat well. Before, when I didn't have money for food, Feroz didn't eat much either. Now her favorite food is croquettes, and maybe she is fat."

Eduardo is hardly alone in faithfully sending money home to Mexico. From less than $4 billion in 1994, remittances climbed to $10 billion in 2002, $20 million in 2005 and, in spite of a major recession in the United States and elsewhere, reached $21.13 billion in 2011.

Would Eduardo have left Oaxaca if there were opportunities for him there? He says no. "I would never leave my daughter and my mother if I didn't have to. And I have a granddaughter now who I have never seen. The idea of the American dream is strong. Yes. But the pull of family and home is stronger. I would choose home every time."

CHAPTER 10

FARMWORKER JESUS

Farmworkers

Farmworkers is the name we give
To the people who work the land,
Who harvest the fields,
United beneath one sky.
Thank you, farmworker,
For the fruits your hands have brought me.
I will grow stronger and kinder
As I eat what you have grown.

Alma Flor Ada

When I think of undocumented workers running across the border, Jesus is who comes to mind. He is young, strong, smart and, above all, hardworking. He passed through my class quietly absorbing English and, the next thing I knew, he was fluent in the language of his new country.

Jesus is like so many we depend on to plant and harvest our food. Without him and other immigrants who work on our farms, the U.S. agriculture sector would collapse. In season, Jesus plants and picks the strawberries, raspberries, blueberries and blackberries that grow so well in our cool, damp northwest climate. In the winter, Jesus performs maintenance doing all those jobs that keep the farm going the rest of the year.

Economic Desperation = Migration

Jesus comes from a family of subsistence farmers in the Mexican State of Oaxaca. His pueblo is in the mountains, not far from Pacific Ocean beaches. He remembers the population of his village as being around 5,000, but a quick search of Wikipedia shows it to be 1,188. Outmigration is a fact of life for many remote Oaxacan pueblos.

Jesus has four brothers and four sisters. His family ground corn for cash income. Trouble began for Jesus' family and other small farmers when the North American Free Trade Agreement (NAFTA) went into effect on January 1, 1994. Customs barriers that previously prevented large U.S. corn producers from dumping their crops in Mexico were removed under NAFTA.

At the same time, NAFTA prohibited the Mexican government from subsidizing family farms (although the U.S. government continued agricultural support programs). As David Bacon and many others have noted, the result of NAFTA in Mexico was that"(i)t became cheaper for larger Mexican corn growers to buy U.S. corn and resell it than to

114

grow the corn themselves." Jesus and his family suffered. Like so many in southern Mexico, they were plunged into extreme poverty.

Jesus' family tried to diversify away from dependence on corn. They grew melons and peanuts and raised chickens, cows and goats. Jesus was happy living on the farm and wanted to stay there and continue in school. There was no money for school and, after primary school graduation, Jesus had to drop out and work on the farm. Then a drought hit southern Mexico, and the corn they raised could not even be fed to the animals. It dried and shriveled on the stalk.

Jesus' oldest sister had already gone north to California, and she urged Jesus to join her. She'd gotten papers under President Reagan's amnesty program, and even though that option was no longer available to migrants who arrived without documentation, it was still relatively easy to cross the U.S./Mexico border. It was 1998, a few years after NAFTA's implementation enabled the flow of cheap commodities from the United States to Mexico. The resulting economic desperation made it necessary for people to migrate north.

Jesus worked in the California fields for four years travelling from farm to farm picking grapes, artichokes, asparagus, onions and garlic. The work was steady for young migrants like Jesus, but he was homesick for his family in Oaxaca, and after a few years he returned to help his father.

Every month, Jesus sent $300 to $400 a month home from his earnings in the United States. Thanks to remittances home, the family kept their farm and even brought in electricity and running water. His family clearly had it better than many others in Oaxaca. But without money from his work in the United States, the family couldn't make ends meet, and Jesus decided to travel north another time.

Crossing the Border Again

In 2005, crossing the U.S./Mexico border was not what it was before September 11, 2001. Jesus paid a coyote $500 to help him cross, and they walked for a day across the hot desert. Jesus was still young and strong, but they ran into immigration, and he was sent back to Mexico. At that time, the U.S. authorities followed a policy of "catch and release" and sent would be crossers back to Mexico rather than detain or incarcerate them. Jesus waited in a church shelter in a border town until he felt it was time to try again. The first coyote would have made a second attempt, but, by then, Jesus had lost faith in him. He hired a different coyote, but the price had gone up to $1000.

Jesus joined the new coyote and a small group of crossers who had also paid the higher fee. This time they walked all night through the desert. Their only light was the moon as they worried flashlights would attract the attention of Mexican officials known to be ruthless with crossers on the Mexican side of the border. Jesus walked all night in the freezing cold of the desert after dark. They passed skeletal remains of those migrants who had not made it. The group paused for a moment at the remains, shuddered, said a prayer and continued on.

Once safely across, Jesus lost no time in heading north. There he joined a friend who was already working in Washington State. He has been there ever since planting and picking berries, fixing and maintaining farmworker cabins, driving tractors and installing irrigation systems.

Jesus is a devout Christian and attends church every Saturday. He, like many others in Latin America, was attracted to evangelical worship and left the Catholic Church. He says his family is about half Catholic and about half evangelical Christian.

It is difficult to imagine that Jesus, a man of faith and a believer in helping his family through his hard work, would become embroiled in a labor dispute that attracted national attention. But that is what happened.

Jesus' Farm: Scene of Labor Problems

The farm where Jesus worked is a big operation, and it is estimated to have an annual income of in excess of $6 million. The farm sits in some of the most beautiful and fertile land in the country. To the west is the Pacific Ocean, and the land itself was reclaimed from the sea. To the east are mountains, which capture the snow that becomes spring melt for summer crops.

The farm is owned by a family with roots in Japan. Some members of the family were interned in California during World War II while others served in the United States military in the same war. They returned to their farm after armistice in 1945 not really knowing what to expect. So many farms of Japanese immigrants had been seized during the war.

In this family's case, neighbors looked after their farm, planting and harvesting the crops and banking the money for the family's return, cementing the family's loyalty to the community to this day. The labor troubles that gripped the farm surprised and divided the community.

Jesus remembers, "The conflict began suddenly, without warning. In July 2013, a worker complained to his supervisor about low piece rates and asked for a raise. He was fired that day. We were shocked, and about 250 of us walked off the fields."

"Problems that had gone on for years came to the surface," Jesus explains. "We wanted higher wages, but we also wanted respect. We wanted to be paid for mandatory break times, and we wanted help with housing costs. Many of us had been with the farm for years, season after season, working hard in the fields. We didn't really want to strike but that's what happened."

Guest Workers: A Sticking Point

Jesus is a modest guy with realistic expectations. "I don't expect to be paid $15 an hour. I'm not a professional. I'm a farmworker. At the same time, I don't want to be replaced with temporary workers. These guest workers are paid more than I am even when we are doing the same jobs." The use of temporary or "guest" workers instead of laborers like Jesus became a major point of contention in the labor dispute.

"It became clear that our jobs were at stake," Jesus told me. "They planned to replace us with temporary workers. These workers have to return to Mexico or wherever they

118

are from at the end of their contracts and are often treated really badly. It was a cheap shot."

In 2013, the farm applied for 160 temporary "guest" workers under the H-2A visa program and brought in about 70 of them. In the spring of 2014, strikers got form letters telling them that they had all been fired. The farm applied for 438 H-2A guest workers, just about the number they need to harvest the berry crops. Strikers wrote to the U.S. Labor Department protesting the move and said that they were available and willing to work. The farm withdrew its application for temporary workers and, for the 2015 season, did not submit another application.

"We are against the temporary worker program," Jesus points out. "To us, it is like the old bracero program, which was ended in the 1960s. Bringing workers here on temporary visas is slavery. Temporary workers are not protected, and they take jobs away from people who are already here. Many of us have been here a long, long time. And, what's to stop temporary workers from just staying on in the United States after their contracts are finished?"

The Future of Farm Work

The labor dispute ended when the farm agreed pay $850,000 which was partly to pay workers for a mandatory ten minute rest break for every four hours of work. All piece-work pickers must take this break but, until then, were not compensated for the time. Also, the farm agreed to hire only locally available workers and provide higher wages, better housing and supervisor training.

The truth is that farm laborers like Jesus are not as readily available as they once were. Immigration is now at net zero because people are less willing to risk crossing the border as Jesus did, and conditions in Mexico are improving. People are trying to stay home. What happened at Jesus' farm may be replicated throughout the U.S. agricultural sector.

In Florida, for example, a coalition of tomato pickers won agreements with 14 major food retailers to improve pay for workers and to eliminate forced labor, child labor and violence and sexual assault of farm laborers. These and other changes are making a big difference in the lives of workers, and their annual pay is now about $17,000 at participating growers versus an average of $12,500 to $14,999 at other growers.

Instead of fanning xenophobia, anti-immigration sentiments across the country, we should be thanking Jesus and his coworkers in our fields and farms. Without them, we might not be eating.

"I like it here now," Jesus tells me. "I'm content with the settlement, and I want to stay on as a year-round, full-time employee. I like the classes at the college, and I'm working on my high school diploma. I have an American girlfriend. The only problem I have is not being able to go home to visit my family because if I go home, I don't think I could come back."

CHAPTER 11

A MAN FOR THE POOR THE PADRE

Thanks

Wind and sky, rain and sun,

Cloud and shade, field and flower

Thank you, Earth

For all your delicious fruits.

Alma Flor Ada

Of all the students I have taught, perhaps the most special was a student in my very first year as an English instructor. My class was funded by the local community college, but it took place in the lunchroom of a local farm.

The class met at night long after farmworkers had eaten and gone back to apartments in town or cabins on the farm.

One night a man in his early forties came to class at the farm. He was nicely dressed as were all the other students. I helped him fill out the form required for registration by the community college. I asked him the usual questions, and then, out of curiosity and to practice speaking English with him, I asked, "Are you married?" He smiled and said no, he wasn't. I asked him if he had children, and again he smiled and said, no. Then he laughed a wonderful, happy laugh. He told me he was the priest at the local Catholic Church. He had recently moved from Colombia and needed English to conduct mass, visit people in the hospital and, if necessary, see them in jail.

The Padre brought joy to our little class. I sensed it was a joy emanating from a deep gratitude. And for a new, inexperienced teacher, he was a gift.

The Padre was no ordinary student. In addition to his native Spanish, he was fluent in Latin and Hebrew, Italian and French, Greek and Aramaic. His move to our quiet, agrarian corner of the United States was by accident. He had been on vacation in the U.S. before he was to be permanently reassigned to a post in Africa, his first choice.

The need for Spanish-speaking priests in the U.S. is great. Only 2,700 of the country's 47,000 Catholic priests are Latino. Especially in agricultural areas of Washington State, where a large percentage of the population is Latino and most are Catholic, the need for Spanish-speaking priests is enormous. The Padre's vacation was interrupted by a job offer which he accepted and moved to Washington State.

A Dangerous Occupation

He came from one of the most dangerous places in the world. San Isidro Labrador Parish in Medellin, Colombia, is the center of the global drug trade and the conflict between the revolutionary armed forces known as FARC and the Colombia military. The Padre faced danger every day in the course of his duties. For priests, Colombia is a very violent place indeed.

"It isn't safe to be a man of the cloth in Colombia," declared the *Iglesia Descalza.* In 2005, "suspected rebels killed two Catholic priests, ambushing their car as they drove down a country road in northeastern Colombia."

The attack was blamed on FARC, a group known for kidnappings, ransom and the production and distribution of drugs. The Colombia Conference of Bishops conference reported that between 1984 and 2011, eight bishops, 79 priests and three seminarians were murdered in the country.

"It wasn't the danger that made me want to leave Colombia," the Padre explained. "It was the frustration. The farmers in San Isidro work so hard at backbreaking labor. They only want something better for their children, but the narco terrorists would show up and demand 'protection money.' Or they would make the famers destroy their crops to plant coca for the production of cocaine."

"It was dangerous for me. I was out there with the farmers, not to be a hero but to be a companion to the people. God helped me many times. I didn't have a problem with the narco terrorists, the guerillas or the

123

communists, but all of them had problems with me and the Church, and so we were often targets."

A Life of Service

"I came from a very poor background myself. My father was badly injured when I was just a kid, and I had to work to help my family. I chopped wood. I went to the market. I did odd jobs to bring home a little cash. Sometimes I would find my mother crying because we had so little for dinner. My entire childhood was helping. Becoming a priest was a natural step for me."

"School was my refuge. I was lucky that I got to go to school. The priests at the school saw I wanted to learn, and they made sure that I could. I studied every minute I wasn't working or helping my family. It was my joy to learn new languages, new subjects, philosophies and history. We didn't have television, of course, or even books in my house. So school was where I found out about the world. In my family, I found out about love. Love is caring for others, but it was in school where I found a love of learning."

"As a teenager, I decided to devote my life to helping the poor and the disenfranchised. I had been lucky. School saved me, but many are not so fortunate. From an early age, I began to see my role in the world as a mediator between the poor and the institutions that are supposed to serve them but don't serve them in reality. The role of the Church is to give people hope through God. The role of the priest is to help people deal with life and find hope."

The Preferential Option for the Poor

The Padre's devotion to the poor has deep roots in the Catholic Church. In the decades of his youth, the 1960s and 70s, the Church adopted the Preferential Option for the Poor and Vulnerable. As reported by the Center for Social Change of the University of Notre Dame, the Option adopted by the Latin American Bishops Conference in Medellin (1968) and Puebla (1979) stated:

As followers of Christ, we are challenged to make a preferential option for the poor, to create conditions for marginalized voices to be heard, to defend the defenseless...From the Scriptures we learn that the justice of a society is tested and judged by its treatment of the poor.

It was in Medellin, so close to where the Padre would work for many years that the movement, known as "liberation theology," was born. By seeking to "apply religious faith by aiding the poor and oppressed through involvement in political and civic affairs," liberation theology put the Church in direct opposition to the very system that creates so many poor people. It was a radical approach. The Church later backed away from this extreme position, but the seed was planted. Some in the Church, like my student the Padre, took his commitment to the poor very seriously.

Poor people have many problems in the complicated conflicts that raged in Colombia between the communists and the government on one hand and the narco terrorists on the other.

"What started in the 1960s as a movement by Marxists to help the poor," the Padre observes, "quickly became the opposite. The poor were caught in the country's many battles and were overlooked, used and abused."

The Padre lived in Medellin for ten years. During that time, the Church tried to negotiate between the various factions involved in conflict in Colombia. "I did what I could to maintain the peace where I lived," the Padre explained. "Even today, the forces continue in opposition. However, the momentum has shifted, and it is quieter now."

From Medellin to the United States

"What I found in Washington was not like the 'war' in Colombia. Planes are not landing in unmarked strips in deep forests. No one appears in the fertile farmland to demand protection money. Priests are not hunted down and shot. The countryside looks serene.

"One reason behind the success of farms here is the availability of cheap and abundant labor from Mexico. Mexicans work in the fields and make more in a day than they would in a week in their native country. They understand and appreciate that, but under the calm rhythm of daily work, there is an undercurrent of fear, illness and pain. That's where my job comes in."

The statistics bear out the Padre's observations. Washington State is a destination for immigrants from many countries and even from within the United States. From about four percent of the State's population in 1990, Latinos are now almost 12 percent. Undocumented workers are over five percent of Washington's workforce. Latinos make up a very high percentage of the student body in public schools.

In many ways, these workers and their children are welcome in Washington State. Until recently, undocumented residents could obtain unrestricted driver's licenses. Further, the State of Washington passed the Real Hope Act providing $5 million additional funds to the State Needs Grant program so that students who want to go to college can get financial aid regardless of their immigration status.

The Dark Side of Immigrants' Lives

Night after night, as his English improved, the Padre told me more about his work. After only six months of classes, he conducted mass in English, and he could help his parishioners in their negotiations with hospitals and the legal system.

In class, students' present bright, happy faces, and when I ask them how they are, they invariably tell me that they are fine, and they smile. These are strong and resilient people, and most are young, under 25.

But the Padre sees the other side of their lives. He goes to their houses and shares their pain. The problems come from many sources. Some employers take advantage of them and cheat them out of their wages. There are landlords who don't provide decent living conditions but charge high rents. Many problems are with the law and the constant fear from living in the United States without legal documentation.

"Of course, there are many problems I can't solve. I pray with the people, and I share with them what resources the Church has. I tell them their rights and what they can do even without legal status in the country. Most of all, I can provide hope."

The Padre can do what no one else can.

"Sometimes, I would go into a home where there were many problems, and I identify a source of the problem. For example, I visited someone who bought a picture at a yard sale and hung it in their living room. The picture looked nice, but it may have brought with it problems from a previous owner. I could see that this picture was having a bad influence on their families. We removed it, and we took it outside and burned it together. To some this act may seem like superstition, but to me and to them, it was a solution. They could face the future knowing that they took action."

A Priest's Role: Exorcism

Today, Pope Francis recognizes exorcisms, which have gone on in the Church for centuries. Pope Francis is credited with an increase in the use of exorcisms to fight the devil's work.

Before Pope Francis assumed office, the Padre was no stranger to this practice. Sometimes, an exorcism was the only answer the Church had to a problem.

"There was a woman possessed by the devil, he told me. "Before, she had been a perfectly normal wife and mother. But then the devil came into her soul. Perhaps it was stress. I don't know. It is always difficult to pinpoint the exact cause of a change in a person's life. But the people around her, her family and people in the Church, could see that she started acting like a crazy person, screaming, pulling her hair, hitting her children."

"Her family called me. I did the only thing I could think of doing. I grabbed her arms and pulled. She carried on. She screamed and cried. I held on as tight as I could. She looked awful, and she was dirty with torn clothes. She hadn't bathed in a week. It was difficult just to hold her arms, but I prayed. I prayed for God's power to hold on. Slowly, she came back to the person she was and is. Her face became normal. She stopped screaming. She hugged her children. Everyone cried. I guess this is called an exorcism, but for me, it was doing the only thing I could think of doing."

Reassignment to the Seattle Area

After several years in rural Washington, the Padre was reassigned to Seattle area.

"People are coming here not just from other countries like Mexico but from other states. They come from Florida, Virginia, California, Arizona and other places looking for work. They started coming here in greater numbers during the 2008 recession. Then they discovered they could get a driver's license, attend English classes and have a better life in Washington State.

"There are many obstacles to adjusting to a new country," the Padre explained. "The growth in the Latino community in the Seattle area means that there's a lot of competition for jobs. Over and over, I'm called in to help people who haven't been paid or where working conditions were very bad. When you are here without papers, you are at the mercy of the system. Even when you have papers, you may not know the language or your rights, and life is not easy."

"People are often attracted to evangelical churches," the Padre continued, "because they seem to promise so much." First generation immigrants are 74 percent Catholic and 15 percent Protestant. By the third generation, a shift occurs, and about 62 percent still identify as Catholic while nearly 30 percent are Protestant.

"When they see that what was promised is not delivered, they often return to the Catholic Church. Part of my job is to welcome them back, especially the youth. For them, the Church can be an alternative to gangs. Today, many, many young people do not have refuge in school as I did. So many bad things have infiltrated the schools that it is not safe for them there."

"And the parents, often working two or three jobs just to get by, are not home to see what their children are doing, whether they are skipping school, joining a gang or using drugs or alcohol. They think they are lucky to have a job or two, and the kids are left to fend for themselves.

"In my work, I meet kids, some as young as 10 or 12, who don't want to live anymore. They are depressed, and they feel abandoned by their parents. They are American, usually citizens born here, but they also feel Mexican. They are caught between two cultures, one very traditional and the other, dangerous and sometimes amoral."

Role of the Church

"The Church must do more," the Padre says. "Families are still the key to everything. However, if the families can't cope and schools are failing, then the Church can and must step in. Very often my role is to simply talk with the parents and their kids. Sometimes I take somewhat of a contrarian approach. People come to me and say that their kids don't want to live at home anymore. They want to be like Americans and move out when they turn 18. I tell them, let the kids move out. But before they leave, tell them to make a list of what it costs to live on your own. After they finish adding up the costs of rent, food and transportation, they often change their minds."

Many people dream of returning to their home countries, but this is a source of generational conflict. Young people usually want to stay here because this is all they know. The hardships and bad economies their parents escaped have not really changed. Dreams of return are often not realistic.

"The American dream of working to provide children with a better life is very much alive in immigrant families," Padre explains. "In fact, unlike much of the country where people are cynical about getting ahead, latinos work against great odds to achieve the American dream for their families. It is important to recognize their contributions. Imagine, if farmworkers didn't work for just one week, the whole economy would fall apart."

A New Pope, a New Beginning

The Padre is deeply encouraged by Pope Francis.

"He is one of us, a Latino. I fully expect that he will make the changes that our Church has to make in order to meet the needs of the people. He has put the poor at the center of his life's work. As an indication of where his heart is, Pope Francis brought to the Vatican Father Gustavo Guitierrez, the founder of liberation theology. His call for social change to recognize the root causes of poverty is a big shift for the Church. But real transformation will depend not just on the Pope but will involve each one of us."

Very recently, Pope Francis said, "The measure of the greatness of society is found in the way it treats those most in need, those who have nothing apart from their poverty."

In a very real sense, the Church is moving back to where it was when liberation theology was adopted and to where the Padre has been all along.

Last year, the Padre celebrated 25 years as a priest. His work on behalf of the poor, which began in Colombia, continues in the United States. He became a U.S. citizen in 2014. Because he defended and helped the disenfranchised in his home country, he ran afoul of some of the most violent elements in what has been a very violent society in South America. For the Padre, Colombia remains a dangerous place. Even on short visits to see family, he is guarded and protected by a ring of loving supporters. He is still vulnerable, even after many years away.

The Padre remains unfazed, "I am committed to devoting my life to those least able to help themselves. To do that, I accept vulnerability and risk."

I am reminded of watching Pope Francis on television as he visits dangerous places around the world and seems to notice only the people who need to see him.

CHAPTER 12

LOVE THY NEIGHBOR VS. XENOPHOBIA

President Reagan once declared, "It is time we stopped thinking of our nearest neighbors – Canada and Mexico – as foreigners." He led the movement towards amnesty for those who had crossed to the United States without papers. The 1986 Immigration Reform and Control Act gave legal documentation to many who were undocumented in the United States. President Reagan might very well be taken aback by the country's inability to deal with the issue of immigration reform, and by the collapse of any bipartisan agreement on what should be done about the 12 million people who are in the country without legal status.

Xenophobia became central to the 2016 Presidential race with then-candidate Donald Trump naming Mexican immigrants as "rapists" and "criminals" and calling for all undocumented people to be deported. He would build a wall along the entire U.S.-Mexican border to keep everyone else out of the country. In late 2018, the Trump Administration even shut down the government over the issue of funding the wall.

At the heart of all debates on immigration is the question of how people are treated both here and in their home countries. In the case of Mexico, immigration to the rich country in the north has been a safety valve in that workers can find jobs by migrating to the United States. For Mexico, workers in the United States have been a source of cash. About 11 percent of Mexico's population now resides in the United States. Their remittances home add up to over two percent of the Mexican Gross National Product. For its part, the United States depends on cheap labor, especially in agriculture. Immigration issues will undoubtedly occupy administrations and congresses for years to come.

A Dramatic Shift in Immigration

The rise in anti-Mexican, anti-immigrant sentiment comes at a time when immigration from Mexico is actually declining, and indeed more Mexicans are leaving than coming to the United States according to the Pew Research Center. No single factor accounts for the reversal in immigration from Mexico. The drop persists even after the U.S. economy continues to recover from the economic recession which began in 2008.

However, the decreasing immigration from Mexico has been accompanied by a sharp increase in migrants from Guatemala, El Salvador, and Honduras. These immigrants from Central America are mostly seeking asylum, and are presenting themselves at the border. (See "A Surge from Central America" below.)

One obvious reason for the decline in undocumented immigration from Mexico is the border itself which is now a formidable barrier. After September 11, 2001, the United States government began beefing up security along the southern border. Between 2004 and 2014, the United States spent $90 billion on border security, more than on all other federal law enforcement activities.

The United States now spends about $14 billion annually for Border Patrol, $6 billion on Immigration and

Control Enforcement (ICE), and $2 billion on detention of migrants. About 700 miles of a so-called fence along the southern U.S. border have already been constructed at a cost of between $4 million and $12 million a mile depending on the location.

Raul Salinas, Mayor of the border town of Loredo, Texas, was quoted in the *Washington Post* as saying, "What used to be an almost invisible barrier became an often insurmountable obstacle." Would-be border crossers are frequently driven to less accessible, more dangerous desert areas in their attempts to reach the United States. As a result, deaths have mounted, usually from dehydration and exposure.

Border enforcement has been monetized and privatized with a Congressional mandate to fill 34,000 beds a night in privately-owned detention facilities. By the end of fiscal 2013, President Obama's Administration had deported 1,951,400 people. Many face lengthy jail sentences if they try to cross the border back into the United States. Punitive approaches to dealing with undocumented crossers and asylum seekers have intensified since the Trump Administration took office.

Border enforcement is not the only reason why immigration from Mexico has declined. Change on the southern side of the border is also a factor. After years of stagnation, the Mexican economy has grown twice as fast as the United States' economy in the post-recession period. Declining birth rates in Mexico and better education throughout the country have reduced pressure to go north for work.

Intangible factors are at work too. Even though over half of Mexico's population is still poor by any monetary measure, a 2012 poll reported in the Seattle *Globalist* showed only 13 percent consider themselves disadvantaged. Some Mexicans are returning to their country of birth or heritage because they miss their culture and families. One recent returnee stated, "Yes, in the United States I could buy more. But I was lonely for my culture and my family still in Mexico. And, I was working so much that I wasn't spending time with my children."

Bernardino Hernandez was featured in the Seattle *Globalist* as a good example of those who've returned to Mexico after feeling limited by a lack of legal status in the United States. He graduated from the University of California at Davis before the DACA program was adopted and couldn't find work. He, like half a million others ages 18 to 35 who have returned to Mexico after spending significant time in the U.S., are sometimes called "*los otros dreamers*," or "the other dreamers." Hernandez went back to Mexico determined to be successful, and he founded a start-up multi-lingual company serving Mexican and American businesses. He achieved the "American dream," but he did it in Mexico.

Immigration in a Time of Turmoil

President Trump did not invent anti-immigrant fervor, but he elevated its status. According to Jorge Ramos, journalist and author, what is new is that "some of the attacks (on foreigners) are coming from the President of the United States himself. Something like this has never occurred before." In June of 2018, President Trump even went so far as to say that undocumented immigrants are "infesting" our country, a term normally used to describe vermin, not people.

Immigration, a hot issue since the beginning of the Trump campaign, continued to grab headlines and emotions throughout 2017, 2018 and into 2019. Major points of contention include:

The fate of **Deferred Action on Childhood Arrivals (DACA)**, commonly known as 'Dreamers,' remains uncertain. President Trump officially ended the program on September 5, 2017, but allowed DACA recipients with a work permit set to expire on or before March 5, 2018, to apply for a two-year extension. The Dreamers were told to use this time to prepare for removal from the country.

The federal courts stepped in to prevent mass deportations of DACA recipients, but their definitive fate awaits Congressional or Supreme Court action. Meanwhile, the futures of some 800,000 DACA recipients and about another million who are eligible for the designation remain in limbo.

In April of 2018, the Trump Administration ordered a **"zero tolerance"** policy of prosecuting all 'unlawful' immigrants as criminals. The zero tolerance policy set up a situation whereby children accompanying their parents are separated when their parents are taken into custody for criminal prosecution. In just the month after announcing this policy, over 2,300 children were taken from their parents.

The zero tolerance policy appears to apply (1) to those attempting to cross the U.S. border without documents for the first time; (2) to those making repeated attempts; and, (3) to those seeking asylum.

In the case of those trying to cross without papers for the first time who do not have a criminal record, they are committing a "mere misdemeanor" in the words of the former U.S. Customs and Border Protection Commissioner Gil Kerlikowske. Those seeking to obtain asylum in the United States are pursuing a legal path to enter the country. Yet all were treated like serious criminals, and their accompanying children were separated from them and locked up as well.

In addition to trying to deter would be crossers and asylum seekers, many observers also think the policy was designed to pressure Congress into accepting changes to immigration law, including funding the wall between the United States and Mexico, changes that they might otherwise oppose. It is unknown what the fate of the children will be, and some may never be reunited with their parents. A firestorm of opposition to this separation policy ensued, and President Trump partially reversed it. Many questions, however, remain unanswered.

The Trump Administration announced the end of **Temporary Protective Status (TPS)** for many immigrants admitted in the wake of natural disasters or protracted unrest or conflict. About 300,000 people have TPS. The majority are from El Salvador, Honduras, and Haiti. However, people from Sudan, Nicaragua, and Nepal also have had their status revoked. About 7,000 people from Syria have TPS, and their status was extended for now.

The so-called 'travel ban' on immigrants from predominantly Muslim countries led to a public outcry in January of 2017 at airports and other places around the country. The original ban was modified, and its third version which included applicants from 'non-Muslim countries' as well was approved by the Supreme Court on June 26, 2018.

Deportation of the undocumented was a recurring theme in the Trump campaign, but has it been a reality? President Trump's anti-immigrant rhetoric has created a climate of fear, and some feel as if a mass roundup is underway. Among noncriminal immigrants, who felt comfortable during the last years of the Obama Administration, deportations are way up. CNN reported that in 2017 arrests of noncriminal immigrants were double that of the previous year.

Changing Immigration: What Does It Mean?

Farmers feel the pinch of a declining workforce first. Farm work in the United States is dominated by immigrants, usually from Mexico. Most of these workers are undocumented. The numbers speak for themselves. According to a study published by the Partnership for a New American Economy aptly titled "A Vanishing Breed," in the decade between 2002 and 2012, the number of new farmworkers coming into the United States fell by 75 percent.

A recent situation in Western Washington may preview what is to come in the agricultural sector. Strikes, walk outs and court action occurred at Sakuma Bros. Farm in Burlington, Washington. It came as a great surprise to nearly everyone in Skagit County that a labor dispute with national attention and implications would happen there. The dispute and the court actions were eventually resolved largely in favor of the workers, primarily because the farm owners didn't want their crops to rot in the fields. There simply isn't a surplus of farm labor to move in and take the strikers' jobs.

Sakuma CEO Dan Weeden reported that in 2011 and 2012, Sakuma left almost a million pounds of berries unpicked in the fields. He said that American workers don't want these jobs. Rather than face uncertainty, in 2016, Sakuma offered to negotiate with a union representing the workers to ensure a supply of labor. On September 13, 2016, Sakuma farmworkers voted 195 to 58 in favor of authorizing the labor group *Familias Unidas por La Justicia* to represent them.

What happened at Sakuma Farm was unusual but not isolated. In 2010, tomato pickers in Florida organized for higher wages and better working conditions. Today 14 major retailers, including Whole Foods, Walmart, McDonalds and Subway, pledge to only work with suppliers who participate in and meet the requirements of the organization known as the Coalition of Immokalee Workers.

Michael Barone, writing for the National Review, said, "The vast immigration from Latin America, mostly from Mexico, between 1982 and 2007 is over -- at least for now." The result, according to Barone, is that "the debate over legalization and/or a path to citizenship will become less relevant over time." What does it mean? Farmworkers may now have greater leverage in labor disputes, but what are the implications beyond these immediate examples?

A recent Forbes magazine article has predicted a "global labor shortage" and international competition for migrants. "People are increasingly becoming a scarce resource, and policies that make a country less welcoming may, in 20 or 30 years, look like China with regard to its one-child policy." In other words, anti-immigration policies may turn out to be self-defeating. The Forbes writer, Brad McMillan, says that misguided policies are already creating problems in the agriculture industry, "Farm labor shortages are common to the point where the agriculture industry has actually called for immigration reform to attract more laborers, not to send them home."

In 2014, a report by the Partnership for a New American Economy, as reported by the New York Times, said that "labor shortages make it impossible for American farmers to increase production and compete effectively with foreign imports." An estimated $1.4 billion in yearly income is reportedly lost to the agricultural sector due to lack of labor.

How changing demographics will translate into public policy is unclear. Charges of labor shortages, especially in the agriculture sector, can be misleading. David Bacon makes the point in his book, **The Right to Stay Home**, that farm owners and others cry shortages in order to make their case for expanded programs that bring in temporary workers.

President Donald Trump's immigration policy would replace the 12 million people he would deport en masse with 'legal' workers. His policy would greatly expand the H-2 temporary worker program, which opens the door for farm and other workers for limited periods of time in sectors where there are 'shortages.'

Sakuma Bros. Farm attempted to use the H-2 temporary worker program during the strikes. This move was met with very stiff opposition from migrant workers who had come to Sakuma year after year, season after season, and worked very hard. They wrote to the U.S. Labor Department that they were available workers and disputed Sakuma's claim that local labor was not available. Sakuma ended its application for temporary workers.

It is not just Republicans who argue over immigration. Secretary of State Hillary Clinton in a Democratic Presidential candidate debate with Senator Bernie Sanders asserted that Sanders had voted against immigration reform. He countered that he wasn't against reform, quite the contrary. He was against the greatly expanded temporary 'guest worker' program contained in the legislation.

However polite the term 'guest worker' may sound, its reality is entirely different. In a landmark study done by the Southern Poverty Law Center in 2013, the conclusion was, "The current H-2 program which provides temporary farmworkers and non-farm laborers for a variety of U.S. industries is rife with labor and human rights violations committed by employers who prey on a highly vulnerable workforce. This program should not be expanded or used as a model for immigration reform."

The report continues, "H-2 can be viewed as a modern day system of indentured servitude." Representative Rangel of New York stated: "The guest worker program is the closest thing I've seen to slavery."

It should be noted, however, that many farmers are embracing the H-2A program, and it is used by about 150 to 200 growers in Washington State alone. In 2014, guest workers numbered more than 12,000 in Washington State which was nearly double the previous year. Supporters of temporary visas for farmworkers say that their minimum wage of $12.69 an hour and perks like free housing bring their hourly wage up to $15 an hour.

Who can guarantee that once workers arrive in the United States for 'temporary' jobs that they won't simply fade into the community and swell the undocumented population? About 40 percent of the people who are here 'without papers' are 'overstayers,' those who entered the country legally as students, fiancés, highly skilled workers, and tourists but overstayed their visas. Congressional Quarterly reports that these people "then remain in the United States illegally, by staying beyond the specified period of admission. These immigrants, who represent many nationalities, are known as 'non-immigrant overstays.'"

Immigration Reform Languishes

Major immigration reform proposals before Congress in recent years continue and expand guest worker programs. They are at the heart of many programs for reform and are typically combined with tougher enforcement at our southern border. Changes to immigration policy are complicated and controversial, and they have died in the past several congresses. Even programs that have wide support, such as the Dreamers' program, languish in Congress.

Well-meaning people sometimes ask me, "Why don't they just come here legally?" The answer is simple: those who can, do. For the vast majority from Mexico, legal immigration is not an option. There are few provisions in our complex immigration system that allow for people from Mexico (and many other countries) to enter the United States and to stay and work here legally.

In 1965, the U.S. Immigration Code was rewritten to emphasize family reunification. However, there are not nearly enough slots allocated to reunite families as there are people wanting to be with their mothers, fathers, husbands, wives, sisters and brothers. One student waited for nine years for his bride to rise to the top of the list so she could join him from Mexico. Another has been waiting for 15 years since her brother first applied to be reunited with her.

For people who crossed the border without legal documentation, it is no longer an easy route to a green card by marrying an American. This route virtually ended for people who entered the U.S. without legal status after 2001. Exceptions are difficult to obtain and often require lengthy stays back in a home country. Realistically, the marriage option is available maily to people who enter with tourist, student or other visas.

A Surge from Central America

A surge of asylum seekers from the Central American countries of Guatemala, Honduras, El Salvador (the so-called 'Northern Triangle' of countries) grabbed headlines in 2017, 2018 and into 2019.

According to the *Washington Post*, the first large wave of immigrants from Central America arrived in 2014. By the end of that year, some 140,000 people crossed the border from the Northern Triangle countries without authorization. In the first eight months of 2018, nearly 91,500 families from Central American were stopped at the border. According to then-Secretary of Homeland Security Nielsen, apprehension of undocumented immigrants (who were mostly seeking asylum) topped 66,000 in February 2019 and were expected to reach 100,000 in March.

The forces of rampant violence and poverty (and even climate change) are pushing these migrants north. The U.S. government has funded Mexican authorities to stop, detain, and deport those who try to transit to the United States through Mexico. However, as the dramatic increases in unaccompanied minors and asylum seekers show, these efforts to stop migration at Mexico's southern border have had very mixed results. In 2017, Mexico detained and deported 76,433 people attempting to cross from Central America.

The Trump Administration's attempt to make people wait in Mexico while their petitions for asylum are pending was barred by a federal judge. That decision was reversed, but could be overturned on appeal. At the heart of the issue is whether it is too dangerous for them in Mexico. Asylum seekers at the U.S. southern border face an uncertain future.

Oaxacan Workers: A Special Story

Impoverished by NAFTA which put at least a million small farmers out of business in the Mexican State of Oaxaca alone, indigenous Oaxacans migrated to Washington State and other parts of the United States to find work. Many pick, plant and ship the food we have come to expect in our grocery stores. They are the Mixtec, Triqui, Zapotec and others who often speak languages that were thousands of years old when Europeans first landed on this continent.

Poverty in Mexico, David Bacon tells us, "is no more evenly distributed than it is in the United States." Poverty is concentrated in the southern states of Oaxaca and Chiapas. Those states are also where there are the greatest numbers of indigenous people.

If we have reached the moment in history where we need farm labor, why not look to our neighbor to the north to see how immigration issues were settled with Canada. According to the 1794 Jay Treaty, also known as the Treaty of Amity, Commerce, and Navigation, First Nation's peoples (indigenous people) living in Canada are guaranteed the right to come and go to the United States without passports or visas. They can work and live in the U.S., and eventually they can collect social security from the U.S. government if they qualify. All they need to do is to have more than 50 percent indigenous blood as certified by membership in a First Nations' tribe. An identification card from that First Nation suffices for 'papers.'

It is time to impose the standards that the Jay treaty drew up for indigenous people from our neighbor to the north to our indigenous neighbors to the south. It has worked well since 1794 when the Jay Treaty went into effect with Canada and continues to work today. Allowing indigenous people from Mexico the same rights as those extended to those living in Canada will not solve the immigration problem, but it could go a long way to righting a wrong. These people are the ones who were arguably most adversely impacted by U.S. trade policy with Mexico, namely NAFTA, and are deserving of some redress.

I travelled to Oaxaca twice. The first time, in 2008, was shortly after a major teacher strike in 2006. The streets were peaceful, but the markets in the pueblos around Oaxaca City seemed empty. Vendors sold their produce, meats and crafts, and children still lingered near their family stalls, but there was a decided absence of working age people.

I returned to Oaxaca in June of 2016, and this time it was in the middle of a second teacher strike that was to have violent consequences. Still, I visited the markets. The vendors proudly told me, "My son is in Atlanta. He's a painter." "My son married an Argentinian. He's living in Argentina." "My children worked in California, and now they are in Washington." And so it went. Their voices were full of hope, but their eyes held tears of longing for their children, many of whom they hadn't seen in years. Going to another country to work and live is often a one-way ticket for those without legal documentation. If people without papers go home, their return to the United States is now extremely difficult if not impossible. Prospects for earning a living have not substantially improved in southern Mexico, and the incentive is to remain abroad and send remittances home even if it means not seeing close family members for long stretches of time.

"Immigrants Get the Job Done"

Lin-Manuel Miranda, creator of the smash Broadway hit, *Hamilton*, told a graduating university class that their "stories are essential." His musical tells the story of Alexander Hamilton, a penniless, orphan immigrant from the West Indies who came to New York and built our financial system and shaped our country. It is, Miranda said (and reported in Buzz Feed), "A story that reminds us that since the beginning of the great, unfinished symphony that is our American experiment, time and time again, immigrants get the job done." It is a line from a song in the play.

The American Dream is all about "getting the job done." It's a dream of working hard, sending your kids to school, maybe buying a house, starting a business and making a difference. The great labor leader Cesar Chavez once said, "We have looked into the future, and the future is ours." Certainly, the demographics bear out his prediction. By November 8, 2016, Election Day, 27 million Latinos were eligible to vote. There are 55 million Latinos in the country today, and that number is expected to reach 125 million by 2050.

Their stories are important. Their dreams are important. A Fox News poll found, "Even in the height of a major recession, Latinos still believe in the American Dream."

There are, however, distinctions in how immigrants view the American Dream. The Hispanic Executive draws this distinction, "In many ways, the Hispanic American Dream is no different from the traditional American Dream...The main distinction is that the dream is not just about the individual, it's about family."

This distinction is not just true for Latino immigrants. In **The True American,** Anand Giridharadas, an immigrant from Sri Lanka, wrote, "We immigrants, when we come to this country, we feel pressure to be successful, to do something good, because of our family teaching that we have to make our parents happy."

Certainly, this sentiment was felt in my own family as my grandparents worked hard and brought over every member of their families, saving them from unthinkable deaths in the hands of dictators. They "got the job done," and so will immigrants and their children who are here today.

Jorge Ramos, in his book **Stranger: The Challenge of a Latino Immigrant in the Trump Era,** stated: "In the end, the demographic revolution that the United States is currently experiencing – in which minorities will become the new majority – will end up overwhelming xenophobia, rejecting the radical extremist groups, and the United States can continue with its tradition of ethnic diversity, multiculturalism, and acceptance of immigrants."

Michael Wildes, immigration attorney to the Trump family, and a former federal prosecutor, quoted the words of the Chief Rabbi of the British Commonwealth, Lord Jonathan Sachs: "Only once does the Bible tell us to love our neighbor. But thirty-six times, the Bible tells us to love the stranger."

Finally, Howard French wrote in the June, 2016, issue of *The Atlantic,* "Immigration, perhaps more than any other single factor, sustains American prosperity." No other powerful country, he noted, assimilates immigrants on a scale matched by the United States.

I like to think that by teaching English to those recently arrived in the country, I am helping them in the assimilation process. I once asked a student whose job it was to mix feed for dairy cattle what his children were doing. He replied that his daughter was in medical school and his son was preparing to enter law school. This student's story is the story of my family and billions of other immigrant families.

SOURCES

Ada, Alma Flor, **Gathering the Sun**, Harper Collins, New York, 1997.

All of the poems heading each chapter about the immigrants are from this book.

Bacon, David, **Illegal People**, Beacon Press, Boston, Mass, 2008.

Bacon, David, **The Right to Stay Home**, Beacon Press, Boston, Mass, 2013.

Both **Illegal People** and **The Right to Stay Home** are excellent sources of information on Mexico and especially Oaxaca, root causes of immigration, and labor issues involving Latinos in Mexico and the United States.

Bacon, David, "Guest Workers as Strike Breakers," *The Nation*, May 2, 2014.

Balk, Gene, "Immigration from Mexico Jumps Here, Bucks Trend," *Seattle Times*, September 10, 2016.

Barron, Michael, "Will the American Dream Hold True for Hispanics?" *National Review*, March 20, 2015.

Bernton, Hal, "Effort to Keep a Workforce Amid Immigration Battles," *Seattle Times*, June 26, 2018.

Bernton, Hal, "Legalize Undocumented Framworkers? Some Republicans Say Yes," *Seattle Times*, July 1, 2018.

Briceno, Norberto, "Lin-Manuel Miranda Just Delivered a Powerful Statement about Immigrants," *Buzz Feed*, May 16, 2016

Carcamo, Cindy, "Raised in the U.S. without Legal Status, He Attains the American Dream – in Mexico," *LA Times*, April 24, 2016.

Cave, Damien, "Deep Ties, Tested on Mexico's Border," *New York Times*, May 11, 2014.

Cornwell, P., "Sakuma Brothers Growers to Pay $850,000 Settlement," *Seattle Times*, June 13, 2014.

Corchado, Alfredo, "The Migrant's Said: Torbio Romo is a Favorite of Mexicans Crossing the Border," *Bandaras News*, July 2006.

Davidson, Adam, "Coming to America," *The New Yorker*, July 27, 2015.

Dockerman, Daniel, Hispanics of Peruvian Origin in the United States, 2009, Pew Research Hispanic Center, May 26, 2011.

Dudley, Mary Jo, "These US Industries Can't Work Without Illegal Immigrants," *The Conversation*, June 25, 2018.

Editorial Board, "Deportees, Then and Now," *New York Times*, September 7, 2013.

Eulich, Whitney, "For Mexico's Migrant Workers, a Push for Cross Border Justice," *Christian Science Monitor*, December 14, 2015.

Eulich, Whitney, "For Mexico's Migrant Workers, a Push for Cross Border Justice," *Christian Science Monitor*, December 14, 2015.

French, Howard W., "China's Twilight Years," *The Atlantic*, June, 2016.

Fox News Poll, "Latinos Believe in the American Dream, Poll Says, " September 15, 2012

Frazelle, Brian, "The Truth about Immigrants: Xenophobia Existed in Early America," *The Houston Catholic Worker*, December 1, 1999.

Giridharadas, Anand, **The True Americans**, W.W. Norton & Co., New York, 2014.

Gjelten, Jon, **A Nation of Nation**, Simon and Shuster, New York, 2015.

Green, Miranda, "Farming, Tech Companies Struggle with Labor Shortages, Want Immigration Reform," www.decode.com, July 15, 2016.

Green, Nicole W., **Immigration**, CQ Press, Washington, D.C., 2002.

Heath, Tom, "American Xenophobia," about.com.

Hullet, Alysa, "Rejecting the American Dream, Mexicans Reintegrate Back Home," *Seattle Globalist*, March 26, 2015.

Iglesia Desclaza, September 14, 2011.

Jenkins, Don, "Sakuma Berry Farm Proposes Vote on Union," *Capital Press*, July 12, 2016.

Kaminsky, Jonathan, "Washington State Real Hope Act," *Reuters*, February 19, 2014.

KFDI, "Immigration Reform," July 15, 2016.

Kruhly, Madeleine, "Is American Identity Rooted in Xenophobia?," *The Atlantic*, June 16, 2012.

KPLU, Seattle, Wa, June 26 2014.

Kulish, Nicholas, "Human Smuggling Cat-and-Mouse Game Plays Out beyond the Border," *New York Times*, July 11, 2018.

Markeiz, Michelle, "The Hispanic American Dream," *Hispanic Executive*, Custom Media, Chicago, IL, 2016.

McMillan, Brad, "What Population and Labor Supply Mean for Immigration, *Forbes*, November 24, 2015.

Mehrotra, Kartikay, "Trump Barred From Forcing Asylum Seekers to Wait in Mexico," *Bloomberg*, April 8, 2019.

"Mexico's National Soccer Team Takes a Stand Against Homophobia in Football," *Huffington Post*, April 4, 2016.

Miller, Todd, **Border Patrol Nation**, City Lights Books, San Francisco, CA, 2014.

Montanaro, Domenico, "Throwback Thursday: Reagan Announces Run for President," npr.org, April 16, 2015.

Nakamura, David, "Beyond the Photos: A Border Crisis that's Bigger than any President," *Washington Post* (as reprinted in the June 24, 2018 *Seattle Times*).

Peck, Don, "America's Emigration Problem," *The Atlantic*, July/August, 2013.

PEW Research Center, 1615 L Street, Washington, DC 20036.

Regan, Margaret, Detained and Deported, Stories of Immigrant Families Under Fire, Beacon Press, Boston, Mass, 2015.

Ramos, Jorge, **Stranger: The Challenge of a Latino Immigrant in the Trump Era,** Vintage Books, Random House, New York, 2018.

Preston, Julia, "Hillary Clinton and Bernie Sanders Draw Distinctions on Immigration Policy," *New York Times*, May 17, 2016.

Schiff, Stacey, "Anger: An American History," *New York Times*, December 18, 2015.

Stone, Brandon, "Sakuma Berry Workers Vote to Unionize," *Seattle Times,* September 14, 2016.

Southern Poverty Law Center, "Close to Slavery: Guest Worker Programs in the United States," February 18, 2013.

Suarez, Ray*n*, Latino Americans: The 500-Year Legacy That Shaped A Nation, the Penguin Group, New York, NY, 2013.

Tobin, Jeffrey, "American Limbo," *New Yorker*, July 27, 2015.

University of Notre Dame Center for Social Concerns, Notre Dame, IN, 2015.

Washington, John, "Border Wall," *The Nation*, May 11, 2016.

Wilkinson, Francis, "Robots Won't Pick Tom Cottin's Strawberries," *Bloomberg News*, March 8, 2018.

Yardley, Jim and Romero, Simon, "Pope Focus on Poor Revives Scorned Theology," *New York Times*, May 23, 2015.